THE ULTIMATE GUIDE TO
INTERNET
RESOURCES
FOR TEACHERS
OF GIFTED STUDENTS

THE ULTIMATE GUIDE TO
INTERNET
RESOURCES
FOR TEACHERS
OF GIFTED STUDENTS

**FRANCES A. KARNES, PH.D.,
& KRISTEN R. STEPHENS, PH.D.**

PRUFROCK PRESS INC.
WACO, TEXAS

DEDICATION

We dedicate this book to all gifted children and youth, to their teachers, and to our families: John, Leighanne, Mary Ryan, Mo, Emma, Brooks, and Betsy and Rich, Karen, David, and Jack for their love and support, and to Christopher and Ray Karnes and Karen and David Stephens for their special love and guidance.

Library of Congress Cataloging-in-Publication Data

Karnes, Frances A.
The ultimate guide to internet resources for teachers of gifted students / by Frances A. Karnes, Ph.D. &
Kristen R. Stephens, Ph.D.
    pages cm
Includes bibliographical references.
ISBN 978-1-59363-969-3 (pbk.)
1. Gifted children--Education--United States--Handbooks, manuals, etc. 2. Internet in education--United
States. 3. Education--Computer network resources. I. Title.
LC3993.9.K373 2013
004.67'8071--dc23
                        2012033075

Edited by Sean Redmond

Cover and layout design by Raquel Trevino

ISBN-13: 978-1-59363-969-3

Printed in the United States of America.

At the time of this book's publication, all facts and figures cited are the most current available.
All telephone numbers, addresses, and websites URLs are accurate and active. All publications,
organizations, websites, and other resources exist as described in the book, and all have been
verified. The authors and Prufrock Press Inc. make no warranty or guarantee concerning the
information and materials given out by organizations or content found at websites, and we are
not responsible for any changes that occur after this book's publication. If you find an error, please
contact Prufrock Press Inc.

Prufrock Press Inc.
P.O. Box 8813
Waco, TX 76714-8813
Phone: (800) 998-2208
Fax: (800) 240-0333
http://www.prufrock.com

TABLE OF
CONTENTS

CHAPTER 1

INTRODUCTION

The Internet has sparked both a social and cultural revolution in our lives. For many, it may be hard to recall what life was like prior to its arrival. According to the National Center for Education Statistics, nearly 100% of public schools in the United States had access to the Internet in 2005, compared with just 35% in 1994 (Wells & Lewis, 2006). These figures demonstrate just how quickly the Internet has become embedded within our culture. With its vast array of content, the Internet continues to grow moment by moment, and is thus a viable means for gifted students to broaden and deepen their knowledge. In fact, Siegle (2005) stated: "The Internet is the single most significant technology available to gifted and talented students" (p. 30).

The Internet provides students with access to the most recent scholarly work in any field. Through video and audio clips; images; books, journals, newspapers, and other traditional media; blogs; e-mail; chat rooms; and discussion boards, students have a wealth of information at their fingertips. In addition, the emergence of Web 2.0 has clearly changed the way users experience the Internet—moving from merely accessing read-only content to actual interaction and engagement with user-created content.

With information on any topic readily available with the click of a button, the Internet presents many unique opportunities and challenges in today's classrooms. This guide is designed to help teachers make better use of the Internet for educational purposes.

Although teachers across all subject areas are the focus audience of this book, counselors, librarians, media specialists, youth organizations, and parents are also sure to find many useful applications for the ideas presented. From tips on how to integrate Internet-based learning experiences into the classroom to methods to help students become informed consumers of Internet content, it is hoped that the information contained here will assist those responsible for preparing students to be wise information creators and consumers in the 21st century.

BENEFITS OF THE INTERNET FOR GIFTED LEARNERS

The Internet has become an essential tool for teachers who strive to deepen and enrich the curriculum for gifted learners. Before the Internet, teachers and students had to make multiple trips to the library to acquire books and resource materials that enabled gifted students to explore certain topics in greater depth. Now, the world's library is accessible within the classroom through a computer and Internet connection.

CURRICULUM ENRICHMENT

Teachers can supplement and/or replace textbooks and other grade-level reading material with more complex and challenging resources found on the Internet. One way of providing gifted students with more sophisticated reading material is through the use of primary sources. For example, a unit on the Great Depression might be supplemented with political cartoons from that era, or records of the Supreme Court on *Brown v. Board of Education* might be explored when studying segregation issues.

The Internet also affords students the opportunity to engage in independent study with relative ease. Independent studies can be facilitated by the teacher through the use of learning contracts or by involving students in WebQuests designed to deepen understanding in content areas. A WebQuest is an inquiry-oriented assignment in which students are provided with a task and a series of web-based resources to explore that have been selected by the teacher. WebQuests can be designed to take anywhere from one day to several weeks for students to complete and can be designed as individual or small-group activities. One of the main benefits of a WebQuest is that students don't have to spend time searching for information on the Internet, as the links they are to use to complete the task are already provided by the teacher. Although WebQuests take time to create, they can be easily updated and used again with future students. Teachers are encouraged to develop a library of WebQuests that are aligned with the curriculum, as they provide an effective way of differentiating for gifted learners.

QuestGarden (http://questgarden.com/search) contains WebQuests that are created by teachers and are organized by content area and grade level. In addition, Bernie Dodge from San Diego State University has developed a WebQuest about WebQuests (http://webquest.sdsu.edu/webquestwebquest.html), which takes the user through the process of understanding the format and function of a WebQuest.

The Internet also affords gifted students the opportunity to engage in online learning. A number of organizations offer online courses specifically designed for children and youth with advanced abilities. Some of the courses are offered synchronously, meaning students participate in live online classes using web-conferencing software such as Adobe Connect (http://www.adobe.com/products/acrobatconnectpro) or Blackboard Collaborate (http://www.blackboard.com/Platforms/Collaborate/Overview.aspx). Other programs offer asynchronous, self-paced classes where students access course materials and assignments at any time through a course management system (e.g., Blackboard, Moodle, Sakai). Following are a few online programs designed specifically for gifted learners.

- *Gifted LearningLinks* (http://www.ctd.northwestern.edu/gll)— Offered through Northwestern University's Center for Talent Development, this online program provides classes for students in grades K–12 in a variety of content areas. Students participate in real-time class sessions, and high school credit is available for some courses.
- *Education Program for Gifted Youth (EPGY) at Stanford University* (http://epgy.stanford.edu)—Offers both synchronous and asynchronous courses for students in kindergarten through college level. The fully accredited Online High School is also an option, offering students in grades 7–12 the chance to earn a diploma.
- *Duke TIP's e-Studies Program* (http://tip.duke.edu/e-studies)— Provides asynchronous courses in a variety of content areas for students in grades 8–12.

For a listing of other learning opportunities for gifted students, including online experiences, see the National Association for Gifted Children's Resource Directory (http://www.nagc.org/resourcedirectory.aspx).

CONTENT EXPERTS AND MENTORS

The Internet provides users with access to other people all over the globe. Through e-mail, chat forums, discussion boards, blogs, and social networking sites, students can easily connect with experts from a whole host of fields or with peers with similar passions, interests, and abilities.

When a gifted student's knowledge in a content area exceeds that of his or her parents and teachers, content experts are critical in sustaining student interest and academic growth. Teachers can locate university faculty or graduate students in a content area through college and university websites or business leaders through corporate and organization websites. Many authors also have their own domains with contact information available. In addition, with the ability to communicate and network online, these content experts no longer have to live within your community—they can be anywhere in the world!

There are also a variety of "Ask an Expert" sites where students can post their most pressing questions within relevant fields. The Howard Hughes Medical Institute hosts Ask a Scientist (http://www.askascientist.org). On this site, students can ask a question, explore answers to the top questions, learn about careers in science, and get homework help. Drexel University manages Ask Dr. Math (http://mathforum.org/dr.math). At this site, students can search the archive for answers to questions at the elementary, middle, high school, and college levels or submit questions of their own.

Many children's authors and illustrators maintain websites with information for teachers and students. These sites allow users to connect with authors as well as with other readers who were inspired by the author's work. A few examples of authors with websites include:

- *Avi* (http://www.avi-writer.com)—Contains a separate teacher section with discussion guides and information on how to arrange a Skype visit with the author.
- *Jan Brett* (http://www.janbrett.com)—Provides a multitude of resources that can be used in the classroom, including links to hundreds of free activity pages based on her books, more than 40 accessible video clips of the author discussing her books, and a blog where students can leave comments for the author.
- *Eric Carle* (http://www.eric-carle.com/home.html)—Through the Caterpillar Exchange Bulletin Board (listed under Resources), teachers and students can share their creative ideas for using Carle's books in the classroom. The site also has an image and video library and hosts an author's blog.
- *Mem Fox* (http://www.memfox.net)—Leave comments for the author, e-mail the author directly, and see and hear Fox read from her books. The site also includes the stories behind her stories and tips for writers.

Looking for a particular author? The Children's Literature Web Guide (http://www.acs.ucalgary.ca/~dkbrown) maintained by David Brown at the University of Calgary provides a list of direct links to hundreds of author and illustrator sites.

The Internet also opens the door to potential mentors for students. Telementoring or e-mentoring programs are available through many reputable organizations. The University of Illinois at Chicago's Women in Science and Engineering (WISE) Pre-College Outreach program (http://www.uicwise.org/outreach) connects middle and high school girls with professional women in science, engineering, and technology fields through the Girls Electronic Mentoring for Science, Engineering, and Technology (GEM-SET) program. Students communicate with their mentors via e-mail. The Electronic Emissary (http://emissary.wm.edu) is a web-based telementoring service that helps K–12 teachers and students locate mentors from a variety of disciplines. Such mentoring experiences can assist gifted students with career exploration and help them begin to formulate their own research questions within a discipline.

Teachers, schools, and districts can establish their own e-mentoring programs for the students they serve. MENTOR: The National Mentoring Partnership (http://www.mentoring.org/find_resources/ementoring_clearinghouse) provides a wealth of information for establishing and maintaining an effective e-mentoring program.

LIKE-MINDED PEERS

There are also websites that connect children and youth with similar interests and passions with one another. Cogito (http://www.cogito.org), developed by Johns Hopkins University and eight other partners, provides students with the opportunity to network with others interested in math and science. Students can engage in online interviews with experts, access information on summer programs and academic competitions, and participate in discussion forums with other students.

Online book clubs offer another way for youth with similar interests to connect. Students can post comments and read those submitted by others who have been inspired by a particular work. Such forums allow students to participate in rich discussions around book themes. Teachers are encouraged to check the websites of their local public libraries to see if they host virtual book clubs for youth.

Avid readers will enjoy Kidsreads (http://www.kidsreads.com), which provides information on a multitude of books and authors, houses a collection of book club discussion guides, and provides tips for starting a book club. The sister site, Teenreads (http://www.teenreads.com), provides similar information for adolescents.

The Internet has virtually (no pun intended!) opened up a whole new world of possibilities for gifted learners. The ability to instantly connect students with the resources they need to deepen their learning is now possible with the emergence of these new technologies. The Internet has clearly changed the way we learn and connect with one another, and as this vast virtual space continues to evolve and expand, new possibilities for its use with gifted learners will certainly emerge.

INTERNET-BASED CLASSROOM TOOLS

Although the Internet is largely used to obtain information and communicate with others, it also has become a primary source for music, movies, news, commerce, and social networking. In addition, the many potential (and realized) educational uses of the Internet are still being explored. In 1999, Gerzog and Haugland introduced four categories of learning opportunities available to students using the Internet:

- information gathering, research, and virtual field trips;
- global communication;
- publishing; and
- interactive sites.

These same learning opportunities are still available today, but as new technologies emerge, teachers and students have even more options for integrating the Internet into the classroom. Specifically, many new tools now exist for the purpose of building online communities. Wikis, blogs, and discussion forums offer users the opportunity to create and share content in ways that move beyond e-mail and other, more limited forms of communication. The emergence of these new tools has converted users from mere consumers of content to actual creators of content. In addition, these tools are simple to set up and use. Gone are the days of having to know HTML coding to create such virtual spaces. Today's tools work very similarly to familiar document management systems (e.g., Microsoft Word); therefore, most individuals find them fairly straightforward and easy to navigate.

The Internet provides teachers with a multitude of tools that can be integrated into lessons to foster student understanding in and across content areas. With access to streaming media (e.g., videos, podcasts), primary sources, and an endless array of images, the Internet can enhance classroom instruction in a variety of ways. Following is a list of some basic instructional tools that are available for free on the Internet with examples of how each can be used in the classroom.

- *Maps*—There are many sites that offer interactive maps suitable for projecting on the classroom wall to generate exploration and discussion. Google Maps (http://maps.google.com) provides satellite and street-level views on most maps. Other sites include MapQuest (http://www.mapquest.com) and Yahoo! Maps (http://maps.yahoo.com). Many of these map tool sites also provide driving directions and calculate mileage or distance between locations. These sites can be creatively embedded in math, science, and social studies lessons. Students can use maps to locate the streets they live on, and by using the zoom feature provided on most sites, they can explore both street-level and aerial views of their communities. What better way to connect students with the content they are exploring?

- *Videos and Animation*—Video clips are a great way to deepen student understanding of abstract concepts. YouTube (http://www.youtube.com), PBS (http://video.pbs.org), Discovery Channel (http://dsc.discovery.com), and BrainPOP (http://www.brainpop.com) are just a few examples of sites that host educational videos and animation. As an additional bonus, BrainPOP provides short, online quizzes for students to complete following the viewing of each animated video. Most clips on these sites are between 5–10 minutes in length and can be quite useful in fostering student engagement with class content. Embedding the use of video and animation in lessons also ensures that instruction is addressing a variety of learning preferences.

- *Time*—Online timers (count down) and stopwatches (count up) are great for helping students monitor their time during group activities and in-class presentations or while engaged in work at centers or stations. Many different sites host these virtual timers that can be displayed on a computer screen or projected onto a wall or screen. A few to explore are Online Stopwatch (http://www.online-stopwatch.com) and TimeMe (http://www.timeme.com). For the official U.S. time, by time zone, students will enjoy exploring The Official U.S. Time (http://www.time.gov). In addition, if you need to determine the exact time or time zone in other areas of the world, timeanddate.com (http://www.timeanddate.com) is a good resource.

- *Weather*—Forecasts from virtually anywhere in the world can be explored, compared, and discussed. Some of the most popular meteorology sites include The Weather Channel (http://www.weather.com), the National Weather Service (http://www.nws.noaa.gov), and the World Meteorological Organization (http://www.wmo.int). If you are exploring other countries with your students, a great way to extend the curriculum and help students better understand the climate and ways of life in different regions of the world is to use online meteorology tools to analyze current weather conditions across the globe. For example, students can examine the mean temperatures and total rainfall by month in certain regions of the world using online weather resources.

- *Images*—Photographs can enrich any lesson by adding further intrigue to the topic at hand. Picture History (http://www.picturehistory.com) provides an online archive of images spanning 200 years of American history. Teachers can find images of Lincoln memorabilia, slave auctions in the south, and the construction of the Statue of Liberty, among others. The Library of Congress (http://www.loc.gov/pictures) also hosts an image archive consisting of photographs, fine and popular prints and drawings, posters, and architectural and engineering drawings. The National Gallery of Art (http://www.nga.gov) provides full-screen images of the museum's collection with corresponding information about each piece and artist. If teachers can't take students to the museum, the museum can be brought into classrooms with a virtual tour.

- *Documents*—Primary source documents can now be perused though the Internet without setting foot in a library archive. The Smithsonian Scrapbook (http://www.siarchives.si.edu/history/exhibits/documents/index.htm) houses letters, diaries, and photographs from the Smithsonian Institution Archives. Artifacts pertaining to the Wright Brothers, the Civil War, and

Robert Goddard, the father of modern rocketry, are all available through this site. The National Archives (http://www.archives.gov) also provides immediate access to some of the nation's most popular primary documents: the Declaration of Independence, the U.S. Constitution, FDR's "Day of Infamy" speech, and the Apollo 11 flight plan, to name a few.

- *Reference Materials*—It's no longer necessary to stock your classroom shelves with 10-pound reference books. The classroom dictionary, thesaurus, book of quotations, and encyclopedias can all be accessed online. Merriam-Webster (http://www.merriam-webster.com), Dictionary.com (http://dictionary.reference.com), Britannica (http://www.britannica.com), and Bartleby.com (http://www.bartleby.com) are but a few of the available options. Some do limit access to certain areas on their sites, allowing full access to subscribers only. However, even as a nonsubscriber, one can still use many of the features and obtain plenty of information. Another resource, Wikipedia (http://en.wikipedia.org), is completely free and openly editable, which means that anyone can write and make changes to the articles. The content on the site is constantly evolving with a new edition created every moment!

- *Language Learning*—The Internet now makes it possible to translate words, phrases, and passages from one language into another with a click of the button. Google Translate (http://translate.google.com) and Bing Translator (http://www.bing.com/translator) are two examples of such websites. In addition, About.com (http://www.about.com) has a series of audio language labs where users can listen to words and phrases being spoken in a variety of languages, including German, French, Italian, Spanish, and Japanese. Enter "language labs" in the search field on the About.com site to locate these audio resources.

- *Virtual Rooms/Conferences*—The Internet also makes virtual schools and classrooms possible. Through these online environments, students can engage with teachers and one another (synchronously and/or asynchronously) from anywhere that Internet access is available. In addition, teachers now have access to experts all over the world and can bring them directly into their classrooms using Voice over Internet Protocol (VoIP) technologies. Skype (http://www.skype.com) can be used to make free video and voice calls, send instant messages, and share documents. Through such Internet-based technologies, students can meet and chat with authors, curators, scientists, and others. Teachers no longer are restricted to having only special guests that live near the school visit their classrooms—they can now invite anyone, any place, at any time! Internet-based conferencing also makes class-to-class and school-to-school projects possible. Other web conferencing technologies to check out include ooVoo (http://www.oovoo.com) and GoToMeeting (http://www.gotomeeting.com).

■ *Wikis, Blogs, and Chat Forums*—Robust class discussions and deeper explorations of course content can occur outside of the classroom through an array of online forums. Teachers can create class Wikis around specific areas of study. A Wiki is essentially a collaborative webpage to which students can continually add and edit content. Groups of students can also work on projects together though the use of a Wiki. Blogs (short for web logs) are web publishing tools that allow users to comment regularly (through writing, video, and/or audio posts) on a topic of interest. Blogs provide an opportunity for students to read and write, collaborate and discuss, and even be mentored. Some free sites for hosting these tools include Blogger (https://www.blogger.com) and Wikispaces (http://www.wikispaces.com). It should also be noted that many of these sites offer free space to educators. The classroom walls disappear with the integration of these powerful collaboration tools!

This is just a sampling of the many tools that have direct application for the classroom. As the Internet continues to evolve, new tools will be developed and new uses for old tools will continue to be invented.

INTERNET SKILLS

The advent of the Internet has made it essential for individuals to develop new literacies. Leu, Kinzer, Coiro, and Cammack (2004) stated the new literacies of the Internet "include the skills, strategies, and dispositions necessary to successfully use and adapt to the rapidly changing information and communication technologies and contexts that continuously emerge in our world and influence all areas of our personal and professional lives" (para. 9). Because so much information is available through the Internet, it is essential to develop skills that help organize and make sense of it all. From crafting thoughtful searches to carefully scrutinizing what is found, the following tips are designed to support one's Internet experiences.

SEARCHING

With the multitude of resources available on the Internet, searching it can be like looking for a needle in a haystack if one does not know how to navigate effectively. There are a variety of search engines from which to choose: Google (http://www.google.com), Bing (http://www.bing.com), and Yahoo! (http://www.yahoo.com), to name a few. Some metasearch engines like Dogpile (http://www.dogpile.com), WebCrawler (http://www.webcrawler.com), and Mamma (http://www.mamma.com) return all of the best results from multiple search engines.

There are also specialized search engines designed for locating specific types of information. Google Scholar (http://scholar.google.com) searches scholarly material like books and journals, USA.gov (http://www.usa.gov) searches government-related materials, FindLaw (http://www.findlaw.com) helps users locate case law and legal documents, and Artcyclopedia (http://www.artcyclopedia.com) searches works of art by title, artist, or museum.

NoodleQuest (http://www.noodletools.com/noodlequest) is a comprehensive tool for determining the best search engine to meet specific needs. Simply answer a series of questions by clicking in the appropriate boxes and the site provides a list of possible search engines to use based on your input.

Once an appropriate search engine has been selected, perhaps the most critical aspect of searching the Internet begins—the selecting and refining of search terms. Schneider (2009) highlighted the following as some of the most important points to consider when crafting search terms:

- *Use correct spelling*—Not all search engines are equipped with a spell check, and an incorrect spelling could greatly restrict the number of sites returned in the search.
- *Use root words*—The singular version of a word will return more hits than the plural version.
- *Use quotation marks*—When searching by phrase, place quotation marks around the phrase. In doing so, the engine will read the search term as a phrase, not as separate words.
- *Use Boolean logic*—Some engines make use of the Boolean logic operators AND, OR, and NOT. Use of these terms with words in your search can either narrow or broaden a search. For example, as of this writing, searching Google for "ratio and proportion" AND "lesson plan" returns more than 20,000 site hits, whereas "ratio and proportion" AND "lesson plan" NOT "grade 9–12" returns less than half that number.

By utilizing these search tips, teachers can greatly improve their efficiency in locating high-quality sites for use in the classroom.

EVALUATING SITES

After the search has been appropriately narrowed, it is now a matter of perusing the returned sites to determine what is and isn't suitable. This can sometimes require considerable scrutiny, particularly if the site is from an unknown source. Care should be taken to ensure that selected sites are accurate and free of bias. Some questions to consider when evaluating sites for potential use in the classroom include:

- Is the sponsor/host of the website credible?
- Is the site updated regularly?
- Is the site free of distracting advertisements, pop-ups, etc.?
- Is the site easy to navigate/use?
- Can you count on the site existing in the future?
- Is the content developmentally appropriate for students?

Along with their students, teachers must also become conscientious consumers of the content found on the Internet.

INFORMATION LITERACY: HELPING STUDENTS BECOME WISE CONSUMERS OF CONTENT

Aside from perusing and selecting sites for use in the classroom, teachers must also help students become information literate. The American Library Association (1998) outlined Information Literacy Standards for Student Learning. These standards state that the student who is information literate:

- accesses information efficiently and effectively,
- evaluates information critically and competently, and
- uses information accurately and creatively.

All of these standards can be effectively addressed by teaching students to be responsible contributors to and consumers of the Internet.

The vast amount of information available on the Internet can be overwhelming to students who are trying to conduct research on a topic. Teachers must help students develop the skills necessary for effectively:

- navigating the Internet,
- evaluating the content they come across (separating the wheat from the chaff), and
- using the information derived from Internet sources.

In essence, students need lenses in which to filter incoming information. The skills necessary to successfully perform such filtering tasks are often not directly taught in classrooms; however, such skills have become essential as more and more students are exclusively using the Internet to obtain information for school projects.

ACCESSING CONTENT

As previously discussed, there are many search engines that can be used to locate desired content. In addition to the search engines suggested for teachers, there are also "kid-specific" search engines designed to return sites suitable for children and youth. Some of the more popular of these search engines include Ask Kids (http://www.askkids.com), AOL Kids (http://kids.aol.com), Yahoo! Kids (http://kids.yahoo.com), KidsClick! (http://www.kidsclick.org), and KidzSearch (http://www.kidzsearch.com). All of these search engines provide family-friendly searches that filter out sites containing content that may be inappropriate for children.

Students should also be taught how to select appropriate search terms that will most effectively and efficiently lead them to the information desired. Questions students should consider include:

- What are the most distinctive words and phrases relevant to the content/topic I am seeking?
- What terms/words would help narrow my topic considerably (e.g., "black holes" vs. "space")?

Students should be taught that using quotation marks around specific phrases and combining words or phrases using Boolean logic (the words AND, OR, and NOT) will further refine a search. If further research/sites are needed, students should be encouraged to search using alternate terms (e.g., using "insect" instead of "bug" or "saxophone" instead of "sax").

EVALUATING CONTENT

Once students have located a collection of sites containing relevant content, they must be taught to critically evaluate the information. A good rule of thumb is to inform students not to believe everything they read online without first considering the source. Kathy Schrock (2002) instructed users to apply the "Five W's" when evaluating the credibility of a site:

1. WHO wrote the pages and are they an expert in the field?
2. WHAT does the author say is the purpose of the site?
3. WHEN was the site created and last updated?
4. WHERE does the information come from?
5. WHY is the information useful for my purpose? (p. 3)

It is essential that students become informed consumers of the content they explore on the Internet. They must learn to be critical of all of the information they encounter online and take the steps necessary to ensure the validity and reliability of the information used to support their research.

USING CONTENT

Another problematic area that has arisen with the expanded use of the Internet is plagiarism. Now more than ever, students have the ability to simply cut and paste content directly from the Internet and use it in their own work. Students must be taught to give appropriate credit for other people's ideas and for any facts and statistics that are not common knowledge.

Teachers should help students learn to distinguish between what is and isn't common knowledge. For example, certain facts that are generally known by many people are considered common knowledge (e.g., George Washington was the first President of the United States). Facts considered to be common knowledge do not require a documented source. However, facts that are not commonly known and ideas that are interpreted from facts (e.g., Washington was hesitant to attend the Constitutional Congress in 1787) require a documented source.

Students also need to understand that paraphrasing is not simply changing or rearranging a few words. Furthermore, if an idea was derived from another source, even if it has been restated in one's own words, the source must still be identified.

The Purdue Online Writing Lab (http://owl.english.purdue. edu) is a great resource for teachers and students who want to learn more about how to appropriately credit sources.

CAUTIONS AND SPECIAL CONSIDERATIONS

Use of the Internet has exploded since the year 2000. The Corporation for Public Broadcasting (2002) reported a 70% growth rate in home Internet use from 2000 to 2002. The study also found preschool children to be one of the fastest growing groups online—jumping from only 6% of children ages 2–5 in 2000 to 35% 2 years later. In terms of time spent online, children ages 6–7 reported being online an average of 5.9 hours/week, whereas teenagers reported spending an average of 8.4 hours/week.

As students spend more and more time enveloped in the wonders of the Internet, teachers and parents share the concern of how to best provide a safe online experience. From concerns over the time spent online, to limiting access to inappropriate content, to protecting students from online predators, the considerations for online safety are many.

SCREEN TIME

With the increase in usage, concerns have also arisen over what constitutes too much "screen time." What effect, if any, is computer use having on the cognitive development of children? Fish and colleagues (2008) found that early computer use in the home had a positive effect on young children's cognitive development. Jackson and others (2007) stated that the more children use the Internet, the more they read. However, it has also been found that computer use is contributing to a more sedentary lifestyle and may be contributing to childhood obesity (Mendoza, Zimmerman, & Christakis, 2007) and ADHD in children (Christakis, 2009). The National Association for the Education of Young Children (NAEYC) and the Fred Rogers Center (2012) recently released technology and interactive media guidelines for young children. These new guidelines recommend caregivers to consider the screen time recommendations from public health organizations and state that teachers should "carefully and intentionally select and use technology and media if and when it serves healthy development, learning, creativity, interactions with others, and relationships" (NAEYC & Fred Rogers Center, 2012, p. 5).

Software can be purchased to help control children's computer usage. Check out TimesUpKidz (http://www.timesupkidz.com), which allows time-of-day and duration limits to be established on computers. Free trials are available.

ONLINE SAFETY

From identity theft to online predators, students should be cautioned and encouraged to follow some fundamental ground rules when surfing the Internet. Some general safety tips that all teachers should share with their students follow.

- Never share personal information (name, address, phone number) without a parent's permission.
- Never arrange a face-to-face meeting with someone you've met online without informing your parents.
- Never send anyone your picture without the permission of your parents.
- If you come across information that makes you uncomfortable, notify your parents immediately.
- Never share your username and passwords with others—even your friends.
- Check with a parent before downloading any software from the Internet.
- Never post anything that could be offensive or hurt someone's feelings online.
- Check with your parents regarding the sites you are allowed to visit and the amount of time you are allowed to spend each day on the Internet.

There are several informational websites that focus on teaching the public about Internet safety. SafeKids.com (http://www.safekids.com) provides information on Internet safety for families. The site contains articles on general Internet safety, cyberbullying, and a family contract/pledge pertaining to online safety. NetSmartz Workshop (http://www.netsmartz.org) has information for parents, teachers, and children about Internet safety. The site offers real-life stories from individuals whose lives have been affected by the Internet as well as short cartoons that address Internet-related issues.

CHAPTER 2

RECOMMENDED WEBSITES IN GIFTED EDUCATION

The following list of annotated websites is an excellent place for teachers to start their Internet journey. From organizations that support the needs of gifted learners to museums' and publishers' websites, teachers are sure to find an abundance of information to facilitate advocacy, planning, and learning.

NATIONAL/ INTERNATIONAL ORGANIZATIONS

AMERICAN ASSOCIATION FOR GIFTED CHILDREN

HTTP://WWW.AAGC.ORG

The American Association for Gifted Children (AAGC) researches and publishes information regarding gifted children to parents, educators, and the general public. The AAGC's primary focus is developing curricula for gifted preschool and elementary school students and advocating for increased access to gifted education services and programs. This organization specifically works toward ensuring equal access to gifted education resources for diverse populations and gifted children from families with limited financial resources. The organization also awards scholarships to gifted students.

ASSOCIATION FOR THE EDUCATION OF GIFTED UNDERACHIEVING STUDENTS

HTTP://WWW.AEGUS1.ORG

The Association for the Education of Gifted Underachieving Students (AEGUS) aims to increase public knowledge of underachieving gifted students in the hopes of enacting change through parents, educators, and other advocates. AEGUS also provides a forum where people can share successful ideas and interventions to help exceptional students achieve their full potential. This site offers a variety of resources on twice-exceptional students and those with special learning needs.

THE ASSOCIATION FOR THE GIFTED

HTTP://WWW.CECTAG.ORG

The Association for the Gifted (CEC-TAG), a division of the Council for Exceptional Children, works cooperatively with agencies, individuals, and families in order to improve educational opportunities for the gifted by sponsoring research and activities that promote gifted education. CEC-TAG also supports professional preparation for educators of gifted students and publishes a journal and newsletter. This site also offers abstracts for articles published in the *Journal for the Education of the Gifted* and position statements on a variety of topics.

COUNCIL FOR EXCEPTIONAL CHILDREN
HTTP://WWW.CEC.SPED.ORG

The Council for Exceptional Children (CEC) is an international advocate for the advancement of education for exceptional students. CEC organizes opportunities for professional development and disseminates information in support of special education. CEC also publishes journals and newsletters regarding classroom practices and legal policies. Information concerning students with disabilities is offered in addition to information about gifted students.

MENSA INTERNATIONAL
HTTP://WWW.MENSA.ORG

Mensa is an international society for people with IQs in the top 2% of the population. This organization aims to identify highly intelligent individuals and provide them with meaningful social opportunities. In addition to boasting national agencies in more than 40 countries, Mensa also offers approximately 200 Special Interest Groups, many of which cater to children and one of which is specifically for teenagers in the society. This site offers a wide variety of resources, including a book list for parents and links to stimulating games for children. The children in Mensa are also invited to contribute to the organization's magazine, *Fred: The Magazine for Young Mensans,* by sending in any writing, jokes, or trivia that they would like to see published.

NATIONAL ASSOCIATION FOR GIFTED CHILDREN
HTTP://WWW.NAGC.ORG

The National Association for Gifted Children is an organization that supports the variety and diversity of gifted and exceptional students.

NAGC's goals include research, advocacy, and professional development. Its extensive website offers information about publications, conventions and seminars, advocacy and legislation, and much more. Parents can also find a wealth of resources, including a directory of summer programs and advice for choosing which one will best suit their child's needs. The journal *Gifted Child Quarterly* is published by this organization.

WORLD COUNCIL FOR GIFTED AND TALENTED CHILDREN
HTTP://WORLD-GIFTED.ORG

The World Council for Gifted and Talented Children offers support for the recognition of gifted children worldwide, research concerning the nature of giftedness, and enhanced educational opportunities for gifted students. This organization also publishes the scholarly journal *Gifted and Talented International* as well as resources for parents on developing their child's potential.

INFORMATION, RESEARCH, AND ADVICE

ALL KINDS OF MINDS®

HTTP://WWW.ALLKINDSOFMINDS.ORG

A private, nonprofit institute affiliated with the University of North Carolina at Chapel Hill, All Kinds of Minds® offers a powerful system of programs for helping children succeed. This organization aims to improve education by educating teachers and administrators on recent developments in the study of how students learn. By improving the way they approach their classrooms, the organization argues, teachers can change the educational system one classroom at a time. The site contains articles and ideas for dealing with students of varying abilities and is geared mostly toward educators, though it offers some information for parents.

CARNEGIE LIBRARY OF PITTSBURGH

HTTP://WWW.CARNEGIELIBRARY.ORG/
RESEARCH/PARENTSEDUCATORS

The Carnegie Library of Pittsburgh offers a wealth of resources for parents, teachers, and librarians. Although the site includes basic information on topics such as Internet safety, the most valuable resources offered are its extensive booklists. Booklists are theme-based and organized into grades K–2 and 3–5; topics cover everything from bats to constellations, body parts, and imaginary gardening. The Bibliotherapy Bookshelf provides listings for young children learning about sometimes-uncomfortable topics ranging from bedtime fears to child abuse and disabilities.

CENTER FOR GIFTED EDUCATION AT THE COLLEGE OF WILLIAM & MARY
HTTP://WWW.CFGE.WM.EDU/PROFESSIONAL.HTM

The Center for Gifted Education (CFGE) at The College of William & Mary develops, tests, and distributes a wide range of curriculum materials. CFGE sponsors three annual events: the National Curriculum Network Conference, the Professional Summer Institute on curriculum and instruction, and the Advanced Placement Institute/Pre-AP Summer Institute. Other programming is held as needed to deal with various state and local needs in different locations.

CENTER FOR GIFTED EDUCATION POLICY
HTTP://WWW.APA.ORG/ED/SCHOOLS/GIFTED/INDEX.ASPX

The American Psychological Association's Center for Gifted Education Policy strives to increase public awareness and understanding of gifted children as well as research new methods of teaching and learning. The CGEP's innovative Catalyst program offers high school seniors the opportunity to work with professionals in the fields of chemistry and art through a one-year mentorship.

DAVIDSON INSTITUTE FOR TALENT DEVELOPMENT
HTTP://WWW.DAVIDSONGIFTED.ORG

The Davidson Institute for Talent Development focuses its efforts on providing social and educational opportunities for profoundly gifted children, those who test within the 99.9th percentile on IQ or achievement tests. The Davidson Institute offers students in its Young Scholars program summer learning opportunities at its THINK Institute, an accelerated public middle and high school experience at the Davidson Academy in Nevada, and scholarships for high school graduates. The Davidson Institute also offers gifted educators the chance to become a part of its Educators Guild and advocacy information on specific state policies regarding gifted education.

GIFTED DEVELOPMENT CENTER
HTTP://WWW.GIFTEDDEVELOPMENT.COM

The Gifted Development Center is a part of the Institute for the Study of Advanced Development, which aims to improve understanding of giftedness and advanced development. This organization focuses on assessment of the highly gifted and offers support groups and individual counseling for the exceptionally and profoundly gifted. This site also provides information regarding the issues faced by gifted adults.

HOAGIES' GIFTED EDUCATION PAGE
HTTP://WWW.HOAGIESGIFTED.ORG

This personally managed website includes extensive information for parents, educators, counselors, administrators, students, and teens. The site provides tools for support and advocacy, curriculum resources, assessment information, and conference information. Resources also include information regarding gender issues, social/emotional issues, home schooling, and much, much more. A section with fun information for students is also available.

THE INSTITUTE FOR RESEARCH AND POLICY ON ACCELERATION
HTTP://WWW.ACCELERATIONINSTITUTE.ORG

The Institute for Research and Policy on Acceleration (IRPA), housed at the Connie Belin & Jacqueline N. Blank International Center for Gifted Education and Talent Development at the University of Iowa, provides teachers, parents, and the general public with information pertaining to acceleration. A variety of resources including policies, reports, bibliographies, and personal stories on acceleration are available on the site. Of particular interest is a report titled *A Nation Deceived: How Schools Hold Back America's Brightest Students,* which highlights the disparity that exists between the research and practices and beliefs regarding acceleration.

INFORMATION, RESEARCH, AND ADVICE

LD ONLINE

HTTP://WWW.LDONLINE.ORG/INDEPTH/GIFTED

LD OnLine is a website about students with learning disabilities and ADHD, and the site's Gifted & LD section focuses on working with twice-exceptional students. The site provides information for parents and teachers interested in the dynamics of self-esteem, stress management, and social skills for twice-exceptional students as well as curricula and teaching methods that can help these students succeed. It also includes a Question and Answer section, forums, and recommended books.

THE NATIONAL RESEARCH CENTER ON THE GIFTED AND TALENTED

HTTP://WWW.GIFTED.UCONN.EDU/NRCGT.HTML

The National Research Center on the Gifted and Talented (NRC/GT) conducts research on giftedness and gifted education through its association with the University of Connecticut. The site includes a wealth of information and links to scholarly research. The NRC/GT's Underachievement Study provides parents and educators with strategies on how to foster gifted students so they can fulfill their maximum potential.

2E NEWSLETTER

HTTP://WWW.2ENEWSLETTER.COM

2e is an electronic publication that aims to promote understanding of twice-exceptional students and what they need to succeed. The newsletter features articles on learning differences, profiles of experts and organizations, insightful columns, research findings, conference information, book reviews, inspiring quotes, and other resources.

UNIQUELY GIFTED
HTTP://WWW.UNIQUELYGIFTED.ORG

Uniquely Gifted is a collection of resources compiled by a contributing editor of the 2e Newsletter. This site is intended for families of twice-exceptional students and the professionals who work with them. Great attention is given to the various special needs of twice-exceptional students and the legal issues and policies that affect them. Resources include articles, support groups, personal experiences, and more.

INFORMATION, RESEARCH, AND ADVICE

PUBLISHERS/ PRODUCTS

CREATIVE LEARNING PRESS

HTTP://WWW.CREATIVELEARNINGPRESS.COM

Creative Learning Press is a publisher focused on providing research and curriculum materials for parents and teachers of gifted students. This company is the publisher of choice for Dr. Joseph Renzulli, the current Director of The National Research Center on the Gifted and Talented. Resources from this publisher place heavy emphasis on hands-on activities and in-depth learning experiences. *The Schoolwide Enrichment Model* and *Curriculum Compacting* are two of the more popular titles available from this publishing company.

THE CRITICAL THINKING CO.

HTTP://WWW.CRITICALTHINKING.COM

The Critical Thinking Co. sells products that will help parents to empower the minds of their children through mathematics, science, language arts, social studies, and more. The core of this curriculum material is critical thinking skills, which encourage students to learn on their own instead of simply memorizing and reciting what they are told. This site also offers test prep guides and software for students in grades pre-K–12.

FREE SPIRIT PUBLISHING

HTTP://FREESPIRIT.COM

Free Spirit is a publisher of learning tools that support children's and young people's social and emotional health. Books offered through this publisher, including the popular *The Gifted Kids' Survival Guide* by Judy Galbraith, provide helpful resources on self-esteem, perfectionism, and conflict resolution. Students, parents, and teachers can all find useful material from this publisher.

GREAT POTENTIAL PRESS
HTTP://WWW.GREATPOTENTIALPRESS.COM

Great Potential Press produces books and videos for parents and teachers of gifted students. Key topics include twice-exceptional students, legal issues, underachievement, and bibliotherapy. This publisher also offers some gifted education books in Spanish.

LOVE PUBLISHING COMPANY
HTTP://WWW.LOVEPUBLISHING.COM

Love Publishing offers a variety of titles related to special education, counseling, and social work. In addition to titles specific to gifted and talented students, teachers and counselors can find information and teaching methods to help children with a wide range of difficulties. The books offered through this company would make great resources for an academic study of giftedness and special needs.

THE NATIONAL ACADEMIES PRESS
HTTP://WWW.NAP.EDU

The National Academies Press (NAP) releases more than 200 books per year on topics related to science, engineering, and health. NAP operates as publisher for the National Academy of Sciences, the National Academy of Engineering, the Institute of Medicine, and the National Research Council. In addition to scientific research, NAP also publishes works concerning science education for teachers and administrators.

PRO-ED
HTTP://WWW.PROEDINC.COM

PRO-ED publishes books, tests, and curriculum materials pertaining to special education and early childhood development. Special attention is paid to learning disabilities and disorders and various therapy and

PUBLISHERS/ PRODUCTS

rehabilitation methods. The testing and assessment resources available on this site—including *GATES: Gifted and Talented Evaluation Scales, SAGES-2: Screening Assessment for Gifted Elementary and Middle School Students–Second Edition,* and *TOMAGS: Test of Mathematical Abilities for Gifted Students*—are particularly notable.

PRUFROCK PRESS
HTTP://WWW.PRUFROCK.COM

Prufrock Press is the nation's leading resource for publications for and about gifted and advanced learners. Teachers can find textbooks, activity books, and other resources to help provide differentiation in the classroom and otherwise improve gifted students' education. This publisher is responsible for *Creative Kids*, the largest magazine written by and for kids in the U.S. The website hosts an informational blog and links for parents and educators.

ROYAL FIREWORKS PRESS
HTTP://WWW.RFWP.COM

Royal Fireworks Press is the world's largest publisher of books specifically for gifted children. Most notably, this publisher features the work of Michael Clay Thompson, author of many books pertaining to teaching language arts. Resources are available for parents, teachers, and students, particularly those involved in homeschooling.

SYLVIA RIMM, PH.D.
HTTP://WWW.SYLVIARIMM.COM

Dr. Rimm is a psychologist, author, and advocate for gifted children; some of her more popular titles include *See Jane Win* and *Why Bright Kids Get Poor Grades*. Dr. Rimm is also available as a speaker for conferences and events, where she offers focused advice regarding gender issues in gifted education as well as larger issues like assessment and underachievement. Her website includes her schedule, information about her books and products, and many other resources for parents and educators.

PUBLISHERS/
PRODUCTS

PROGRAMS FOR STUDENTS

ADVANCE PROGRAM FOR YOUNG SCHOLARS

HTTP://ADVANCE.NSULA.EDU

ADVANCE is a 3-week residential program at Northwestern State University in Louisiana. It offers a challenging and rewarding curriculum for gifted and talented students entering grades 8–12. Students enroll in a single course for 3 weeks of in-depth study, covering the equivalent of a year's worth of high school material or a semester's worth of college material. Courses range from logic and chemistry to film studies and Shakespearean drama.

AMERICAN REGIONS MATHEMATICS LEAGUE

HTTP://WWW.ARML.COM

The American Regions Mathematics League (ARML) holds an annual national mathematics competition for students in grades K–12. ARML's annual competition is held simultaneously at four sites: Pennsylvania State University, The University of Iowa, The University of Georgia, and University of Nevada, Las Vegas. Teams of 15 students compete in a variety of individual and group competitions. This website also provides a listing of various math awards and scholarships available to competing students and links to other state, regional, and national mathematics competitions.

BELIN-BLANK INTERNATIONAL CENTER FOR GIFTED EDUCATION AND TALENT DEVELOPMENT

HTTP://WWW.EDUCATION.UIOWA.EDU/BELINBLANK

The Connie Belin & Jacqueline N. Blank International Center for Gifted Education and Talent Development at The University of Iowa offers a variety of programs throughout the year for gifted students. Challenge Saturdays and the Weekend Institute for Gifted Students (WINGS) are available to students during the school year, and the Invent Iowa curriculum offerings guide students in grades K–12 "from idea to patent." During the summer, a range of programs are available for students in grades 2–11, including Challenges for Elementary School Students (CHESS; grades 2–6) the Blank Summer Institute (FLSI; grades 6–8), and the National Scholars Institute (NSI; grades 9–11).

CANADA/USA MATHCAMP
HTTP://WWW.MATHCAMP.ORG

Canada/USA Mathcamp is an intensive 5-week summer program for high school students interested in mathematics. Its goals are to inspire, motivate, teach, and support students who love mathematics. Students can study college-level mathematics, even to the graduate level. Mathcamp is held on a different college or university campus each year.

CARNEGIE MELLON INSTITUTE FOR TALENTED ELEMENTARY AND SECONDARY STUDENTS
HTTP://WWW.CMU.EDU/CMITES

The Carnegie Mellon Institute for Talented Elementary and Secondary Students (C-MITES) offers a number of summer and weekend classes for gifted students. Classes previously offered include Action-Packed Engineering, Advanced Creative Writing, and The Science of Harry Potter. This site also includes testing information for the Elementary Student Talent Search and a wide range of links for students.

CENTER FOR BRIGHT KIDS
HTTP://WWW.CENTERFORBRIGHTKIDS.ORG

The Center for Bright Kids (CBK) is a regional talent center for the Rocky Mountain area. It hosts an academic talent search program based on above-level testing and optimal match. Monthly activities throughout the school year are available for those who have been identified as gifted and talented. Residential summer programming is also available for students in grades 4–11 who are interested in enrichment study or rigorous academic study, depending on the grade level. CBK also offers a mentoring program that matches students in grades 9–11 with professional scholars in their respective fields of interest.

CENTER FOR GIFTED EDUCATION
HTTP://COE.LOUISIANA.EDU/CENTERS/GIFTED.HTML

The Center for Gifted Education at the University of Louisiana at Lafayette offers summer enrichment programs for academically, creatively, and artistically talented students. The Summer Enrichment Program is for students in grades K–8 and offers classes on topics such as jewelry design and entomology. The Summer Scholars program focuses on students in grades 7 and 8 and has hosted classes such as Typography, Viking Sagas, and the History of Comic Books.

CENTER FOR GIFTED EDUCATION AT THE COLLEGE OF WILLIAM & MARY
HTTP://EDUCATION.WM.EDU/CENTERS/CFGE/

The Center for Gifted Education at The College of William & Mary houses enrichment programs for gifted and talented students during summer and winter sessions. Focusing on the Future is a career conference offered for students in grades 6–12, and the Saturday and Summer Enrichment Programs offer classes in science, mathematics, humanities, and the arts for students in grades K–9.

THE CENTER FOR GIFTED STUDIES AT WESTERN KENTUCKY UNIVERSITY
HTTP://WKU.EDU/GIFTED

The Center for Gifted Studies at Western Kentucky University provides opportunities for gifted and talented young people in grades 1–10. Super Saturdays is a 4-week program offered twice a year that offers classes on topics that range from sports science to improvisational comedy, sign language, and fashion, for students in grades 1–8. The Summer Camp for Academically Talented Middle School Students (SCATS) is designed for students in grades 6–8, and the

PROGRAMS FOR STUDENTS

Summer Program for Verbally and Mathematically Precocious Youth (VAMPY), offered through a cooperative agreement with the Duke Talent Identification Program, provides educational opportunities for students in grades 7–10.

DRURY UNIVERSITY CENTER FOR GIFTED EDUCATION
HTTP://WWW.DRURY.EDU/SECTION/SECTION.CFM?SID=150

The Drury University Center for Gifted Education in Springfield, MO, offers summer programs for students in grades K–12, with both residential and nonresidential options. Specific classes are offered for specific grade ranges: for example, students in grades 2–3 can take classes like Toy Box Physics and Everyday Science, while those in grades 4–5 can choose from Video Production: Short Film and R2D2: Research, Robots, Design, Discovery, among others. The Drury Leadership Academy Program helps prepare high school students for college-level classes and even offers students in grades 9–12 the opportunity to earn college credit by taking a class called Living the College Life, which aims to acquaint them with the intricacies of college social life and healthy living.

DUKE UNIVERSITY'S TALENT IDENTIFICATION PROGRAM
HTTP://WWW.TIP.DUKE.EDU

Duke University's Talent Identification Program (Duke TIP) searches for and identifies gifted and talented students in 16 south-central states and then offers multiple support services for those students. Duke TIP offers a number of educational programs in the summer in addition to distance studies and independent learning opportunities during the year. Its *Educational Opportunity Guide* is particularly notable because it allows students to search for programs nationwide according to program type, academic field, location, grade/age level, term, and cost.

FIRST ROBOTICS COMPETITIONS
HTTP://USFIRST.ORG

For Inspiration and Recognition of Science and Technology (FIRST) sponsors student robotics competitions worldwide. The Junior FIRST LEGO League is a noncompetitive program for students in grades K–3. Students in this competition respond to a specific research question or topic and make a "Show Me" poster in order to inform the community of what they have learned. The FIRST LEGO League for grades 4–8 is a team robotics design competition, and the FIRST Tech Challenge for grades 9–12 allows students the opportunity to compete for college scholarships in a slightly larger robotics design competition. The FIRST Robotics Competition is an intensive robotics design scholarship competition for grades 9–12. In this competition, teams of 25 or more raise funds and build a robot that competes in a series of sporting events.

FRANCES A. KARNES CENTER FOR GIFTED STUDIES
HTTP://USM.EDU/KARNES-GIFTED

The central purpose of this center, located at The University of Southern Mississippi, is to further the education of gifted students and those with leadership abilities through teaching, research, and service. Education programs include the Saturday Gifted Studies Program in the spring semester for students age 4–grade 12. The Summer Gifted Studies Program is a one-week residential program offered for students in grades 4–8, and the Summer Program for Academically Talented Youth is a 3-week residential program offered for students in grades 7–10. The Leadership Studies Program provides students in grades 6–11 the opportunity to strengthen their skills as leaders in their communities. The center also offers a career conference for girls in grades 7–12, a parenting conference, and a Day of Sharing for teachers of the gifted.

PROGRAMS FOR STUDENTS

GIFTED EDUCATION RESOURCE INSTITUTE
HTTP://WWW.GERI.EDUCATION.PURDUE.EDU

The Gifted Education Resource Institute (GERI) at Purdue University conducts research regarding psychology of the gifted and effective educational practices for these individuals. The institute provides three youth talent development programs for high-ability children and teens. Super Saturdays offer supplementary educational opportunities for students age 4–grade 8 during the fall and spring semesters. GERI's Super Summer program provides children in grades pre-K–8 challenging learning opportunities and a healthy social environment. The Summer Residential Camp offers commuter and residential options for students who've completed grades 5 and 6. Students who've finished grades 7–12 can also participate in the Summer Residential Camp (residential only), where they can study subjects such as quantum physics, logic, and journalism. GERI also has a diversity initiative that offers scholarships to students from underrepresented groups, including those with minority status, those from lower socioeconomic backgrounds, and twice-exceptional students.

GIRLS ADVENTURES IN MATHEMATICS, ENGINEERING, AND SCIENCE
HTTP://WIKI.ENGR.ILLINOIS.EDU/DISPLAY/
GAMES/G.A.M.E.S.+CAMP

Girls Adventures in Mathematics, Engineering, and Science (GAMES) is a one-week summer camp for academically talented girls in grades 6–12. This camp aims to promote the greater entry of girls and young women into science and engineering fields. At this camp, girls can study bioengineering, chemical engineering, civil engineering, robotics, electrical engineering, environmental engineering, or aerospace engineering. Emphasis is placed on hands-on activities and demonstrations.

HAMPSHIRE COLLEGE SUMMER STUDIES IN MATHEMATICS

HTTP://WWW.HCSSIM.ORG

Hampshire College Summer Studies in Mathematics is a rigorous 6-week-long math program for high school students. Students choose one larger "maxi" class that surveys a larger field, such as probability or graph theory, and they then supplement their study with two more specific "mini" classes, which focus on topics such as number systems, game theory, and linear algebraic methods in combinatorics. Participants are expected to spend a major portion of each day, Monday–Saturday, actively engaged in learning, doing, and sharing mathematics.

INTEL SCIENCE TALENT SEARCH

HTTP://WWW.SOCIETYFORSCIENCE.ORG/STS

In the Intel Science Talent Search competition, high school seniors submit independent research projects to compete for college scholarships. This prestigious award often identifies future leaders in science and engineering, and the foundation has numerous notable alumni including seven Nobel Prize Laureates. Recent winners have submitted projects with topics such as software for spacecraft navigation, classification of fusion categories in mathematics, and molecular mechanisms in cancer cells.

INTERNATIONAL BACCALAUREATE ORGANIZATION

HTTP://WWW.IBO.ORG

The International Baccalaureate Organization (IBO) programs work with schools, governments, and other organizations to develop rigorous academic programming with the goal of preparing students to enter the "rapidly globalizing world." The Primary Years Programme targets children ages 3–12 in developing critical thinking skills and methods of inquiry. The Middle Years Programme for students ages 11–16 teaches how to connect academic studies with experiences in the real world and culminates in a large, independent project. The Diploma Programme for students ages 16–19 includes three core ini-

PROGRAMS FOR STUDENTS

tiatives in addition to traditional coursework. These initiatives are an in-depth independent study in the student's area of interest, a course on the theory of knowledge, and a service-based project that requires students to learn by doing, most notably by working on a larger community project. There are more than 1,000,000 IB students at more than 3,000 schools in 143 countries. The website gives the history of the program, samples of curricula, a profile of the students, and both national and international opportunities for participation.

JACK KENT COOKE FOUNDATION
HTTP://WWW.JKCF.ORG

The Jack Kent Cooke Foundation was established to help students with financial need reach their full potential. It runs several scholarship programs, including the Young Scholars Program, which awards students who demonstrate financial need personalized scholarships to support educational endeavors throughout their high school careers. Students apply to the Young Scholars Program in grade 7 and enter the program in grade 8. Approximately 60 students are selected each year to participate.

JOHNS HOPKINS UNIVERSITY'S CENTER FOR TALENTED YOUTH
HTTP://WWW.CTY.JHU.EDU

John Hopkins University's Center for Talented Youth (CTY) is a talent search program that connects students to gifted education programs nationwide. This website provides an extensive list of online courses, summer programs, and other resources. The CTY Talent Search Parent Network allows parents to communicate with each other about their CTY experiences. The Family Academic Programs are notable because they allow the entire family to participate in the interactive learning experiences of gifted and talented students at museums, aquariums, and research institutions nationwide.

NORTHWESTERN UNIVERSITY CENTER FOR TALENT DEVELOPMENT

HTTP://WWW.CTD.NORTHWESTERN.EDU

The Center for Talent Development offers talent identification services, research, and advocacy in addition to educational programming for gifted and talented students. Summer programming is available for students age 4–grade 12, with residential options available for those in grades 4 and above. Accelerated Weekend Experiences offer grades 5–8 intensive classes in a single subject area, while the Saturday Enrichment Program allows students age 4–grade 9 to study one or two classes over a course of 2 months. Gifted LearningLinks offers students an array of online distance-learning options, including classes that can be used for AP and university credit.

PROGRAM IN MATHEMATICS FOR YOUNG SCIENTISTS

HTTP://MATH.BU.EDU/PEOPLE/PROMYS

The Program in Mathematics for Young Scientists (PROMYS) at Boston University is a 6-week summer program that aims to provide mathematically talented high school students the chance to explore the subject in greater depth while surrounding themselves with like-minded peers. First-year students are enrolled in a number theory class, while returning students may participate in their choice of advanced seminars; past offerings have included The Analytic Class Number Formula, Algebra, and Geometry and Symmetry, among others.

SCHOOL OF MATHEMATICS CENTER FOR EDUCATIONAL PROGRAMS (MATHCEP)

HTTP://MATHCEP.UMN.EDU/UMTYMP

The School of Mathematics Center for Educational Programs (MATHCEP) at the University of Minnesota offers multiple outreach programs to increase education opportunity in mathematics. The Saturday Enrichment Program during the school year allows students in grades 5–7 to take classes on subjects such as topology, non-Euclid-

PROGRAMS FOR STUDENTS

ean geometry, and game theory. The annual Math/Science Fun Fair offers students hands-on demonstrations and presentations in a variety of fields. The Girls Excel in Math (GEM) initiative is designed to encourage girls' enthusiasm for mathematics by providing outreach programs throughout the school year. GEM specifically targets girls in grades 4–7. The University of Minnesota Talented Youth Mathematics Program (UMTYMP) offers highly accelerated courses specifically designed to provide students with an intense academic experience that will stimulate their mathematical interests and abilities. Students from grades 5–7 are identified and recommended by their schools to be eligible for UMTYMP, where they begin at the algebra level.

STANFORD UNIVERSITY'S EDUCATION PROGRAM FOR GIFTED YOUTH

HTTP://EPGY.STANFORD.EDU

Stanford University's Educational Program for Gifted Youth (EPGY) develops and offers multimedia computer-based distance-learning courses. High-ability students of all ages can get individualized instruction, with optimized content and pace. Levels range from kindergarten to undergraduate. The EPGY Online High School (OHS) offers both full-time and part-time options, giving students the option of using the OHS to provide their primary educational career or to simply supplement their other educational pursuits.

WISCONSIN CENTER FOR ACADEMICALLY TALENTED YOUTH

HTTP://WCATY.ORG

The Wisconsin Center for Academically Talented Youth (WCATY) offers an array of programs, ranging from summer residential programs, to grant-funded mentor-guided research projects, to internship opportunities and contests. The Young Students Summer Program (YSSP) is a one-week residential summer program for students who've finished grades 4–6. The Summer Transitional Enrichment Program

(STEP) is a 2-week residential summer program for grades 7 and 8, and the Accelerated Learning Program (ALP) is a 3-week residential summer program for students in grades 9–12. WCATY also offers online learning classes, which can be utilized as co-op classes by schools that wish to offer their students greater advanced learning opportunities.

PROGRAMS FOR STUDENTS

SUPPORT NETWORKS

GIFTED HAVEN
HTTP://WWW.GIFTEDHAVEN.NET

Gifted Haven is a forum for gifted teens with a focus on understanding. Students are encouraged to discuss their successes and difficulties through a variety of peer interactions. Specific topics range from artistic endeavors and reading recommendations to debates of educational policy and jokes and games. Discussions also target topics such as dating, depression, and interaction with parents.

GIFTED HOMESCHOOLERS FORUM
HTTP://WWW.GIFTEDHOMESCHOOLERS.ORG

The Gifted Homeschoolers Forum is a place where students and their families can explore a network of homeschooling information and resources, specifically targeting gifted education. This organization also aims to increase awareness of the needs of gifted homeschoolers and to advocate on their behalf when necessary. Resources regarding twice-exceptional students are abundant on this website.

GT WORLD
HTTP://GTWORLD.ORG

GT World is an online support community for parents of gifted and talented children. It focuses on issues such as parenting and advocating for gifted children and teaching them how to advocate for themselves; the experience of growing up gifted; obtaining an appropriate education; helping gifted students with learning disabilities; and a wide range of other topics. The website also supports a very active mailing list with topics specifically related to homeschooling and twice-exceptional students.

MY GIFTED GIRL

HTTP://WWW.MYGIFTEDGIRL.COM

My Gifted Girl is an online community with the goal of inspiring and offering support for gifted and talented girls and women. This community offers a wide variety of services for students, parents, and educators. Students can interact with their peers, play educational games, learn college and career information, and connect to mentors in their subjects of interest. There is also a section specifically focused on gifted arts.

SUPPORTING EMOTIONAL NEEDS OF THE GIFTED

HTTP://WWW.SENGIFTED.ORG

Supporting Emotional Needs of the Gifted (SENG) aims to help gifted individuals accept themselves and to understand that they are not alone and that they are valued within society. SENG focuses primarily on the impact adults (parents, educators, etc.) have on the lives of gifted children. SENG provides information on identification, guidance, and effective ways to live and work with gifted individuals. Sponsored activities include an annual conference for parents, educators, and health professionals; parenting groups; and webinars. SENG also sponsors National Parenting Gifted Children Week in the hopes of raising awareness of the emotional and social needs of gifted children.

TAG FAMILIES OF THE TALENTED AND GIFTED

HTTP://WWW.TAGFAM.ORG

TAG Families of the Talented and Gifted (TAGFAM) is a support group specifically for parents and family members of gifted individuals. This group uses mailing lists to share stories and advice regarding both the highlights and difficulties of raising gifted children. Administrators encourage individuals to participate as little or as much as needed as a variety of circumstances often dictate the capacity of individuals to contribute to the group.

SUPPORT NETWORKS

LESSON PLANNING RESOURCES

GENERAL

42EXPLORE

HTTP://42EXPLORE.COM

42eXplore serves as a starting point for creating new lesson plans. It offers links to lesson plans and educational programming in addition to annotated links to outside resources. These resources are available for general themes as well as traditional subject areas (English/language arts, fine/performing arts, applied arts, health and fitness, math, science, and social studies). Although it is no longer regularly updated, the information available is useful and the website is particularly easy to browse.

A TO Z TEACHER STUFF®

HTTP://WWW.ATOZTEACHERSTUFF.COM

A to Z Teacher Stuff® hosts a number of lesson plans that are organized by subject area and grade level. Educators can also find printouts and worksheets for students as well as tools for making worksheets and puzzles. There is a forum for discussion and tips on classroom management and working with parents or families, and visitors can subscribe to a free newsletter.

BRAINPOP EDUCATORS

HTTP://WWW.BRAINPOP.COM/EDUCATORS/HOME

BrainPOP Educators is a free section of the BrainPOP website that offers educational resources for teachers. The emphasis of this website is multimedia and technology integration in the classroom. Resources can be searched by subject, grade level, and academic standard. Registration is free, and those new to the site can watch video tutorials in order to acquaint themselves with the layout. Webinars and an educators blog are also available.

BYRDSEED
HTTP://WWW.BYRDSEED.COM

Byrdseed is the personal website and blog of Ian Byrd, a gifted educator. It includes instructional resources for language arts, math, science, and technology. Emphasis is placed on how to incorporate technology into the classroom, and one section is dedicated to addressing the social and emotional needs of gifted students.

CHARACTER COUNTS!
HTTP://CHARACTERCOUNTS.ORG/RESOURCES/INDEX.HTML

CHARACTER COUNTS! is dedicated to character building and ethics education in the classroom. Resources are targeted to strengthen the "Six Pillars of Character" (trustworthiness, respect, responsibility, fairness, caring, and citizenship). Lesson plans are organized according to age, subject area, or Pillar of Character. Information is also available on educational standards. The Honor Above All program aims to stop cheating, and a number of school violence resources are available. There is also a section for parents, and educators can find links to related online resources.

THE CRITICAL THINKING COMMUNITY
HTTP://WWW.CRITICALTHINKING.ORG

The Foundation and Center for Critical Thinking aims to improve education at all levels by presenting publications, conferences, workshops, and professional development programs. By emphasizing instructional strategies, Socratic questioning, critical reading and writing, and higher order thinking, The Critical Thinking Community hopes to reform traditional education. This organization is actively involved in assessment, research, quality enhancement, and competency standards.

THE CURRICULUM PROJECT

HTTP://WWW.CURRICULUMPROJECT.COM

The Curriculum Project provides elementary, middle, and high school educators with training, materials, and software designed to increase student achievement. Its two main initiatives are the Model Classroom Project and the Curry/Samara Model. Both of these projects aim to improve teaching practices in order to ensure the success of students of all abilities. Emphasis is placed on dynamic instruction with curriculum guided by content, thinking, product, assessment, facilitation, and reflection. Software training is available through the website to help bolster these initiatives and implement their core strategies.

EDSITEMENT! THE BEST OF THE HUMANITIES ON THE WEB

HTTP://EDSITEMENT.NEH.GOV

EDSITEment! was created in partnership by the National Endowment for the Humanities, the Verizon Foundation, and the National Trust for the Humanities. It hosts a number of lesson plans and other educational resources that are divided into four categories: art and culture, foreign language, history and social studies, and literature and language arts. In addition to these main categories, the Picturing America and We The People sections (located under the Lesson Plans tab) explore American history through art and enhance the study of American history and culture, respectively. Within these categories, educators can search for resources by grade level, subtopic, and length of lesson plan. Some resources include printable worksheets. Educators can also find a listing of websites recommended for classroom use in addition to a database of student interactive web activities.

EDUCATIONAL RESOURCES AND LESSON PLANS

HTTP://WWW.CLOUDNET.COM/~EDRBSASS/EDRES.HTM

This is the personal website of Dr. Edmund Sass, a professor of education at the College of Saint Benedict/Saint John's University. Dr. Sass offers a large listing of individual online lesson plans in addition to lesson planning resources. Plans are organized according to subject, topic, and theme. There is also a section that offers lessons directly geared to gifted and talented learners.

FEDERAL RESOURCES FOR EDUCATIONAL EXCELLENCE
HTTP://WWW.FREE.ED.GOV

Federal Resources for Educational Excellence (FREE) serves as a database of federal resources relevant to K–12 lesson planning. This website is well organized by subject area and easy to search or browse. Primary documents, photos, videos, and animations are available in a variety of subjects. This database is strong in the arts, the sciences, and especially in U.S. history. The U.S. history resources are organized according to topic and time period.

FLOCABULARY: HIP-HOP IN THE CLASSROOM
HTTP://WWW.FLOCABULARY.COM/TEACHER-LESSONPLANS

Flocabulary is a revolutionary teaching technique that incorporates hip-hop into traditional subject areas in the hopes of motivating learning and creative expression. Not only are hip-hop lyrics emphasized as a form of creative writing, but these lyrics are also seen as a mnemonic device to help students remember facts and themes in other subjects. Resources are divided into four categories: literature, math/science, social studies, and vocabulary. There are also resources that focus on SAT vocabulary. Free songs and videos are available for download or classroom streaming.

I LOVE THAT TEACHING IDEA!
HTTP://ILOVETHATTEACHINGIDEA.COM

I Love That Teaching Idea! is a website where teachers can post successful lesson plans and teaching resources to share with other educators. Resources are available for subject areas (math, science, etc.) and for other teaching-related topics, such as assessment, classroom management, field trips, and substitute teaching. Because these resources are posted by teachers and not directly monitored, the length and quality of each entry varies greatly, but some entries are very useful.

LEARNING EXCHANGE FOR TEACHERS AND STUDENTS THROUGH THE INTERNET
HTTP://COMMTECHLAB.MSU.EDU/SITES/LETSNET

The Learning Exchange for Teachers and Students through the InterNet (LETSNet) offers lesson plans in art/music, language arts, foreign language, health/sports, math, science, and social studies. By going to the View by Subjects section, visitors can browse according to topic and grade level. These lesson plans can be easily adapted for gifted classrooms.

REGIONAL EDUCATION LABORATORY PROGRAM
HTTP://IES.ED.GOV/NCEE/EDLABS

The Regional Educational Laboratories, sponsored by the Institute of Education Sciences (IES) at the U.S. Department of Education, work with school districts and state departments of education on data collection and research initiatives. Ten regional labs exist nationwide. Links to each regional lab are provided and educators are encouraged to peruse the research priorities and reports for their respective laboratories for further resources and information.

PBS TEACHERS
HTTP://WWW.PBS.ORG/TEACHERS

The Public Broadcasting System's website includes a wide variety of resources for teachers of students in grades pre-K–12. Resources are organized based on grade and subject area. The subjects included are the arts, health and fitness, reading and language arts, math, social studies, and science and technology. Activity packs allow educators to add PBS widgets to their own personal sites, and teachers are encouraged to develop their own class websites. Peer connection resources are also available for coaches, educators, and mentors, as are other professional development opportunities.

PEACE CORPS

HTTP://WWW.PEACECORPS.GOV/WWS/EDUCATORS

The Peace Corps website offers a wealth of information for educators emphasizing diversity, multiculturalism, and global awareness. Resources are organized according to grade level, subject, region, and country. In addition to traditional subject areas, there is also information on how to incorporate service-learning projects into the curriculum. Also offered are a number of foreign language resources, including information on Kenyan sign language and podcasts in Arabic, Russian, Bambara, French, Mandarin, Thai, and Ukrainian.

SCHOLASTIC

HTTP://WWW.SCHOLASTIC.COM/
TEACHERS/TEACHING-RESOURCES

The Scholastic website offers a number of lesson planning resources. Lesson plans are organized according to grade level, subject, and calendar. Printable worksheets, assessment information, and a rubric maker are available as well as online activities for students and an easy-to-navigate class homepage builder. This collection of K–12 resources is particularly strong in literacy and language arts areas. The TeacherShare social network offers educators a chance to collaborate with their colleagues.

THE SOCRATIC METHOD: TEACHING BY ASKING INSTEAD OF BY TELLING

HTTP://WWW.GARLIKOV.COM/SOC_METH.HTML

This article by author and educator Rick Garlikov discusses how to incorporate the Socratic method into a more contemporary classroom. The idea behind the method is that, by teaching solely through the use of questions, students can become more active participants in the learning process. A transcript of a math lesson utilizing this method provides an example of successful implementation.

SMITHSONIAN EDUCATION

HTTP://WWW.SMITHSONIANEDUCATION.ORG/

The Smithsonian Institution's education website includes sections dedicated specifically to educators, parents, and students. The educators' page includes lesson plans for pre-K–12 classes on a very wide variety of topics, and they can be searched by grade level, subject, and standard. There is also an e-newsletter, field trip information, and professional development opportunities. The website hosts a resource library that includes links to specific online museum exhibits, documentaries, and other resources. Parents can find interactive ways to highlight their children's education through a trip to a Smithsonian museum. There are also recommended reading lists, printable activity sheets, and a page that highlights other museums and exhibits nationwide. The student section of this website focuses on the topics of art, culture, history, and science. Independent study is encouraged in the IdeaLabs, and the Secrets of the Smithsonian section allows students to explore the history of the museum and the stories of various significant acquisitions.

TEACHABLEMOMENT

HTTP://MORNINGSIDECENTER.ORG/TEACHABLE-MOMENT

A project of the Morningside Center for Teaching Social Responsibility, TeachableMoment is dedicated to encouraging critical thinking on current events and issues. The site includes hundreds of issues-oriented resources and lessons. Resources are searchable by topic area, subject matter, grade level, and/or keyword, and educators can also find a section on teaching strategies for covering controversial topics in the classroom. Classroom discussion is crucial when using these materials, and educators can find resources on how to properly facilitate discussion and debate.

TEACHERLINK

HTTP://TEACHERLINK.ED.USU.EDU

TeacherLINK hosts a database of lesson plans created by students and faculty of Utah State University. The majority of them focus on social studies, with topics emphasizing diversity, globalization, human rights, and other issues. The lessons are organized by topic as well as by grade level. The AFRICA: It's Not a Country unit is particularly notable due to its vast array of resources for curriculum units.

TEACHERS NETWORK
HTTP://TEACHERSNETWORK.ORG

Teachers Network offers a multitude of resources to assist teachers with instructional design. A lesson plan database that can be searched according to subject area and grade level and elementary, middle, and high school curriculum units across a variety of subject areas are available. How-to articles, videos, and online courses can also be accessed through the Teachers Network to support the professional development needs of educators, with topics ranging from Blogging in the Classroom to Supporting English Language Learners, among others.

TEACHNOLOGY
HTTP://WWW.TEACH-NOLOGY.COM

TeAchnology offers lesson plans, rubrics, and other instructional resources for teachers, including a vast collection of printable worksheets organized by subject and topic. Educators can also find evaluation tools and planning information. Of particular interest are the WebQuests, which are organized by content area. Teachers can also create their own WebQuests using the WebQuest Maker. Although some resources require a fee to access, a wide variety of information and tools are available for free.

TEACHERSPAYTEACHERS
HTTP://TEACHERSPAYTEACHERS.COM

TeachersPayTeachers is a website where educators can post their own successful lesson plans to share with their colleagues. Although some resources cost money, more than 40,000 are available for free. These resources can be browsed according to keyword, grade level, subject area—including gifted and talented—and type. There is also a community blog where educators can network.

TEACHING TOLERANCE

HTTP://WWW.TOLERANCE.ORG

Teaching Tolerance is a website operated by the Southern Poverty Law Center that focuses on teaching tolerance in the K–12 classroom. Content is integrated with traditional subjects and resources are organized according to grade level and subject. Free education kits and magazine subscriptions are available for teachers, librarians, school counselors, and administrators. An online archive of the magazine is also available.

THINKFINITY

HTTP://WWW.THINKFINITY.ORG

Thinkfinity makes available a broad selection of free resources related to K–12 education. Educators can find hundreds of interactive activities and lesson plans arranged according to grade level and subject area. Resources can be searched for by keyword or browsed by state curriculum standards. The science, technology, engineering, and math (STEM) resources are particularly notable. Scholarly journals and information regarding conferences and professional development are also available.

TRIBES LEARNING COMMUNITY

HTTP://WWW.TRIBES.COM

Tribes is an organization dedicated to promoting caring, safe, and comfortable learning environments. By reimagining the classroom as a model home, this teaching style creates an active and understanding learning community. Specific resources are available exploring topics such as conflict resolution and leadership cultivation, as are example lesson plans. This site also provides suggested bibliographies and information about funding and grants opportunities. Professional and staff development opportunities are also available.

UNITED NATIONS CYBERSCHOOLBUS
HTTP://CYBERSCHOOLBUS.UN.ORG

The United Nations Cyberschoolbus offers lesson plans for students ages 10–18. Topics include discrimination, the environment, health, human rights, peace, poverty, urbanization, and women's rights. Briefing papers are available for students who are interested in learning about these issues; each includes an overview and sections on progress that's been made and what to do next, among others. There is also a database of information regarding the countries involved in the United Nations (UN). Educators can guide students through a virtual tour of the UN, and there are videos explaining current events and issues worldwide. A WebQuest is available to teach students about child soldiers, and with the Stop Disasters game (found at http://www.stopdisastersgame.org), students can learn about the kinds of infrastructure necessary to protect certain regions from natural disasters.

YALE-NEW HAVEN TEACHERS INSTITUTE
HTTP://WWW.YALE.EDU/YNHTI/CURRICULUM/

The Yale-New Haven Teachers Institute has archived curriculum units developed by their Fellows since 1978. Although the archives are a bit cumbersome to search, there is a great variety of material here, and the units can be browed by topic or under broader conceptual themes by year. Sample unit topics include The Wonders of Bacteria, Accountability and Reconstruction after the United States Civil War, Visualizing Biography: Engaging Your Students' Creative Potential through Graphic Novels, and The Mathematics of a Warming Arctic. Most of the units are for high school students, but could be adapted for use with gifted students of younger ages.

ENGLISH, LITERACY, AND LANGUAGE ARTS

ACADEMY OF AMERICAN POETS

HTTP://POETS.ORG

The Academy of American Poets has compiled a comprehensive list of resources regarding poetry and poetry education. This website includes specific lesson plans on topics such as the poetry of war, women's poetry, and poetry translations. Full-text poems are also available for educators, and some of these poems include an audio reading by the author. Attention is paid to the examples that can be used by educators to demonstrate form, lyric, narrative, irony, and social/historical context. This organization is the force behind National Poetry Month and the National Poetry Read-a-Thon, an ongoing project that encourages teachers to have students read a poem each day for a month, then record 75–100-word responses to different elements of the poems. Teachers can submit the students' responses, which are then cataloged online so that students and educators can see the ways in which students react to certain pieces of poetry.

AYN RAND EDUCATION

HTTP://AYNRANDEDUCATION.COM/
TEACHER-RESOURCES.HTML

Ayn Rand Education is dedicated to exploring the works of Ayn Rand. Educators can find lesson plans and activities for teaching *Anthem*, *The Fountainhead*, and *Atlas Shrugged*. In addition to offering free teacher kits, this website offers free classroom novel sets for secondary educators committed to incorporating Rand's work in their curriculum. Emphasis is placed on various philosophical themes throughout the novels. Details on the Ayn Rand Institute's student essay contests can also be found here.

CARNEGIE LIBRARY OF PITTSBURGH

HTTP://WWW.CARNEGIELIBRARY.ORG/RESEARCH/
PARENTSEDUCATORS/EDUCATORS

The Carnegie Library of Pittsburgh offers educators a wealth of information regarding literacy and reading for elementary students. In addition to booklists, it offers lesson plans, thematic programs, and a list of library services. The Bringing Libraries and Schools Together (BLAST) initiative offers educators the chance to improve their own library facilities as well as engage students in interactive literacy activities. The Super Science @ Your Library program provides reading materials and hands-on experiments to help students learn about topics such as recycling, inventions, and machines.

INTO THE BOOK

HTTP://READING.ECB.ORG/INDEX.HTML

Into the Book is a K–4 reading comprehension program that incorporates eight key strategies: utilizing prior knowledge, making connections, questioning, visualizing, inferring, summarizing, evaluating, and synthesizing. Free video clips are available online for students and educators, and educators in Wisconsin can incorporate entire episodes of the related television series, which is broadcast on Wisconsin Public Television. Those in other states can still use the free online resources to create their own lesson plans. Educators can also find information on how to design and manage a successful classroom setting.

JUNIOR GREAT BOOKS

HTTP://WWW.GREATBOOKS.ORG

Junior Great Books utilizes a shared-inquiry approach to literature. Students develop critical thinking, reading, and listening skills in addition to speaking and writing ability. The Socratic method is emphasized through a critical examination of the Great Books series, which offers age-appropriate reading material for K–12 students in literature, poetry, science, history, and social studies. Educators can also find discussion questions and other curriculum planning tools.

LITERATURE LEARNING LADDERS
HTTP://EDUSCAPES.COM/LADDERS/INDEX.HTML

Literature Learning Ladders aims to integrate literacy and literature with technology. It hosts a number of lesson plans that include content standards, student activities, and links to online resources. Sections focus on topics such as Newbery and Caldecott award winners and graphic novels. This website also offers information on how to create new "ladders" to connect technology and language arts.

NATIONAL COUNCIL OF TEACHERS OF ENGLISH
HTTP://WWW.NCTE.ORG

The National Council of Teachers of English is dedicated to enhancing the teaching and learning of English and language arts at all levels of education. Teaching standards and lesson planning resources are available for elementary, middle, and secondary school teachers. This website offers valuable booklists and summer reading information. The anti-censorship center offers information and resources for educators encountering a censorship issue in their schools. The National Gallery of Writing is a searchable archive of thousands of creative writing projects, organized from pieces written to celebrate the National Day on Writing.

NATIONAL PUNCTUATION DAY
HTTP://NATIONALPUNCTUATIONDAY.COM

National Punctuation Day is a celebration of correct punctuation. The focus is on making punctuation fun in order to facilitate greater literacy and improved written communication. A list of style books and guides is available on the website. Students are also encouraged to identify and correct signs in their communities that use incorrect punctuation. The website includes lots of information and photos, and teachers of young students can book a performance of Punctuation Playtime for their classes.

OUTTA RAY'S HEAD

HTTP://HOME.COGECO.CA/~RAYSER3

Outta Ray's Head is the personal website of retired secondary school teacher Ray Saitz. It hosts a number of lesson plans organized into four categories: literature, poetry, writing, and library science. In addition to these lesson plans, there is also a listing of links to related online resources.

PROJECT GUTENBERG

HTTP://WWW.GUTENBERG.ORG

Project Gutenberg is a searchable site index of literature and media. This site catalogs classic and contemporary works with expired copyrights and makes them available for public use. Educators can find ebooks, audio books, CDs, and DVDs related to a wide variety of topics. This site also includes a depository of digitized sheet music that can be useful for classrooms studying music.

READWRITETHINK

HTTP://WWW.READWRITETHINK.ORG

ReadWriteThink is an extension of the Thinkfinity program that focuses on literacy and language arts. K–12 lesson plans are organized by grade level, type, theme, and objective. Activities and lessons that correspond with the time of year are also available. Educators can find printable worksheets and interactive student activities. Afterschool and rainy day activities are available for parents as well.

THE READING GENIE

HTTP://WWW.AUBURN.EDU/ACADEMIC/
EDUCATION/READING_GENIE

The Reading Genie is the personal site of Dr. Bruce Murray at Auburn University. It emphasizes a scientific approach to teaching literacy. Lesson plans are available for educators of early readers. The collection is strong in its phonics, literacy, and reading comprehension resources.

READING LADY

HTTP://WWW.READINGLADY.COM

Reading Lady is the personal website of literacy coach Laura Kump. This site focuses on K–6 readers and offers an assortment of assessment guides and rubrics. The Readers Theater section is particularly notable for its large collection of scripts available for classroom reproduction. The Mosaic e-mail group is also hosted by this website in order to facilitate teacher collaboration.

SCRIBBLING WOMEN

HTTP://WWW.SCRIBBLINGWOMEN.ORG/HOME.HTML

Scribbling Women offers resources on female American writers. Specific resources include radio dramas based on novels and short stories by celebrated authors. Educators can also find a section that explains how to teach using radio dramas. In addition to valuable audio resources, this website offers a number of lesson plans as well as a free newsletter.

STORY ARTS

HTTP://WWW.STORYARTS.ORG

Story Arts is dedicated to storytelling and increased understanding of oral traditions. Emphasis is placed on speaking, listening, reading, and writing. Resources at this site include activities, games, and student projects suitable for elementary-level language arts curricula. Resources lend themselves to interdisciplinary study with folktales, mythology, and family history.

STUDENT NEWSPAPER PROJECT

HTTP://ED.FNAL.GOV/LINC/FALL95/PROJECTS/
BUTCHER/INTERNETPROJECT2.HTML

Ann Butcher, an elementary teacher from Nicholson Elementary School in Illinois, has created this set of lesson plans, which offer instructions on how to initiate a student newspaper project for students in grades 4–6. After identifying the various parts of a newspaper, students are given individual and group assignments in order to create their own newspaper.

UNIQUE TEACHING RESOURCES

HTTP://WWW.UNIQUETEACHINGRESOURCES.COM

Unique Teaching Resources is the personal website of elementary school teacher Heidi McDonald. Educators can use McDonald's examples to help create their own lesson plans and can download some free, imaginative resources that McDonald has created. Resources here target reading comprehension and written expression, with a particularly strong collection of writing prompts and journal ideas.

WEB ENGLISH TEACHER

HTTP://WWW.WEBENGLISHTEACHER.COM

Web English Teacher is a database of online resources, lesson plans, and activities for K–12 language arts educators. It boasts an extensive collection of literary analysis materials, and there are sections devoted to vocabulary, grammar, mythology, and creative writing. This website's resources regarding media studies and technology integration in the classroom are also noteworthy. AP class resources are available.

WRITE ON! TEACHING MATERIALS

HTTP://WWW.WRITEONPUBLISHING.COM

Write On! Teaching Materials were developed by Heather Glass for students in grades 4–6. These materials guide students through the step-by-step process of revising, illustrating, and publishing their own unique books. Educators can order a kit, which includes all the necessary materials for both students and instructors. After completing the program, students will have produced their own 2" x 3", 4" x 5", or 6" x 9" hardbound book.

LESSON PLANNING RESOURCES
ENGLISH/LANGUAGE ARTS

FINE AND PERFORMING ARTS

8NOTES.COM

HTTP://WWW.8NOTES.COM

8notes.com is an online database of sheet music and lessons for more than 20 different instruments. These resources are organized according to instrument, composer, style, and difficulty. The website also hosts a blog as well as many different forums where musicians can ask each other questions and have other music-related discussions.

ARTS TOOLKIT

HTTP://WWW.KET.ORG/ARTSTOOLKIT

The Arts Toolkit provides a number of resources in dance, drama, music, and the visual arts. Click on a field of interest to access K–12 lesson plans, organized according to grade level. The Idea File offers a wide variety of activities and mini-lessons that relate to the full lesson plans. Assessment tools and multimedia resources are also available. Resources at this site are free, but registration is required to view full content.

ARTSALIVE.CA

HTTP://WWW.ARTSALIVE.CA/EN/RESOURCES/TEACHERS.ASP

ArtsAlive.ca provides a collection of links for music, theater, and dance curricula. This website hosts a number of simulations, manipulations, WebQuests, and online exhibits in addition to audiovisual downloads. Lesson plans accompany all of these online resources, and special collections include resources on theatrical costumes, set design, and performing arts posters.

ARTSONIA

HTTP://WWW.ARTSONIA.COM/TEACHERS/LESSONPLANS

Artsonia serves as a forum of lesson planning ideas, where educators can share successful curricula and build new ideas through collaboration. The site offers resources for students in grades K–12, organized by grade level, medium, and subject. After registering with the website for free, educators can access these resources, which include step-by-step tutorials on how to build an online school art gallery and how to send an online school newsletter. Contests and awards are also available for students whose artwork is posted online, and there is a section specifically for parents.

ARTSWORK

HTTP://ARTSWORK.ASU.EDU

ArtsWork is an initiative sponsored by Arizona State University that offers instructional resources for grades K–12 in the fields of dance, music, theater, and visual arts. Sample lesson plans are available for a variety of topics including political cartooning, original monologues, improvisation, and quilting, among others. Assessment and evaluation tools are also available, as is arts advocacy material and information regarding national and state curriculum standards.

BLICK

HTTP://WWW.DICKBLICK.COM/LESSON-PLANS

Blick hosts a number of lesson plans for students in grades K–12 and special education organized according to grade level and discipline. Video lesson plans and how-to videos are also available. Other resources include an educators forum, a section on teacher news, and Art Room Aid, a page devoted to funding school and community art projects. Blick also sells art supplies, and a school discount can be arranged.

CRAYOLA

HTTP://WWW.CRAYOLA.COM/FOR-EDUCATORS.ASPX

Crayola's website includes more than 1,000 free lesson plans, which can be incorporated into curricula from early childhood to grade 12. These lesson plans are easily searchable by age level, theme, and medium. Student artwork is exhibited online in a virtual art gallery, and mini-grant opportunities are available from this company and its sponsors.

A section of the website is devoted to incorporating art into the curricula of students with special needs. Integrating arts education with other subject areas is also emphasized; one section, for example, shows how art can be used to explain scientific topics such as color and light.

CREATIVE DRAMA LESSON PLANS
HTTP://WWW.CHILDDRAMA.COM/LESSONS.HTML

This website provides performing arts lesson plans organized by age level, type, and content. A particularly notable number of resources focus on improvisation and pantomime. This website also offers an array of material on how to incorporate performing arts into social studies, science, and language arts lessons.

DRAMA RESOURCE
HTTP://DRAMARESOURCE.COM

Drama Resource offers different strategies and techniques for use in drama and theater classes. This website is particularly helpful for its list of games and activities that can be used as warm ups, ice breakers, and tools to enhance group dynamics. Appropriate age range, time needed, and learning objectives are provided for each. Multimedia resources are encouraged, and many links to audiovisual examples are presented.

EDUCATION AT THE GETTY
HTTP://WWW.GETTY.EDU/EDUCATION/
TEACHERS/INDEX.HTML

The J. Paul Getty Museum in California offers art-centric lesson-planning resources for K–12 classrooms. An image bank of paintings and/or other works from the museum accompanies each lesson plan. Lesson plans also include content standards for California public schools, and information is available for building new lesson plans. The TeacherArtExchange is an online community in which art teachers can share ideas, resources, and networks and online games, videos, and activities are available for students to explore.

EDUCATIONAL THEATRE ASSOCIATION

HTTP://SCHOOLTHEATRE.ORG

The Educational Theatre Association (EdTA) and the International Thespian Society, EdTA's student honorary division, work to advance students and educators in the field of theater. Resources on acting and production are available for students and educators. An extensive list of college theater programs and scholarships is also available. Educators can find script resources and information regarding conferences, festivals, and professional development.

INCREDIBLE ART DEPARTMENT

HTTP://WWW.INCREDIBLEART.ORG

The Incredible Art Department is a database of pre-K–grade 12 lesson plans, organized by grade level, medium, subject, art period, and artist. These lessons include WebQuests, booklists, tutorial videos, and other related materials. Resources are also available on how to integrate art with other disciplines. Cartooning lessons are available for advanced artists. This website also offers evaluation and assessment tools.

THE KENNEDY CENTER ARTSEDGE

HTTP://ARTSEDGE.KENNEDY-CENTER.ORG/EDUCATORS.ASPX

The Kennedy Center ArtsEdge challenges teachers to transform their instruction with arts-integrated resources for K–12 classrooms. It includes standards, lessons, and multimedia resources for teachers. Educators can find ways to integrate dance, music, theater, and the visual arts into a variety of other subjects such as history, science, and foreign language. Advocacy tips and resources for arts education are also available.

KINDERART

HTTP://WWW.KINDERART.COM

KinderArt hosts pre-K–grade 12 lesson plans in the visual arts as well as a section on how to introduce students to the culinary arts. Lessons are organized by discipline and grade/age level, and cover topics such as seasonal crafts, multicultural art, and recycling projects. In addition to an e-newsletter and a blog, this website offers a section devoted to arts in special education classrooms. The collection of printables and coloring sheets on this site is particularly useful.

LA OPERA
HTTP://WWW.LAOPERA.COM/EDUCATION/TEACHERS

LA Opera hosts lesson plans for more than 25 popular operas. These lessons are geared toward advanced music students in grades 6–12. Emphasis is placed on reading an opera as a text, with the performance and music enhancing the text. These lesson plans could be incorporated into a number of interdisciplinary classes including creative writing, literature, media studies, music, and visual arts. These lessons include assessment tools and have been aligned with relevant California curriculum standards.

NATIONAL ART EDUCATION ASSOCIATION
HTTP://WWW.ARTEDUCATORS.ORG

The National Art Education Association (NAEA) is the leading professional organization for art educators, researchers, administrators, and museum educators. This organization offers information on advocacy, grants, and other funding opportunities as well as lesson planning guidelines. Assessment tools, content standards, and art experimentation ideas are also available, as is a gallery of students' work.

NATIONAL ASSOCIATION FOR MUSIC EDUCATION
HTTP://WWW.NAFME.ORG

The National Association for Music Education (NAfME) is one of the world's largest arts education organizations and the only association that addresses all aspects of music education. NAfME offers educators lesson planning guidelines and sheet music resources. Advocacy and public policy is also highlighted, in addition to information on grants, scholarships, and funding.

LESSON PLANNING RESOURCES FINE/PERFORMING ARTS

NGA CLASSROOM
HTTP://WWW.NGA.GOV/EDUCATION/CLASSROOM

The National Gallery of Art (NGA) provides interactive lessons that are designed to use art as a way to learn about other subjects. For example, students can study life in the 19th century, discover mathematical patterns, investigate architecture, and explore concepts like heroism, all through the study of famous artworks. Interactive activities and worksheets are also provided, and NGAkids offers games and activities for students to explore on their own. The National Gallery of Art also provides a loan service that allows schools and classrooms to borrow teaching materials from the museum at no cost.

PE CENTRAL
HTTP://PECENTRAL.ORG/LESSONIDEAS/
DANCE/DANCEINDEX.ASP

PE Central offers a wide variety of dance lesson plans and ideas. These resources for K–12 classrooms are organized by grade level, category/subject, and lesson type. Emphasis is placed on integrating dance with other school subjects, such as math and science. This website also provides links to video examples of the activities. Assessment ideas are available for educators as well as variations and adaptations of activities to accommodate students with disabilities.

ROCK AND ROLL HALL OF FAME
HTTP://ROCKHALL.COM/EDUCATION

The Rock and Roll Hall of Fame offers more than 50 lesson plans concerning the history and significance of rock and roll in American society. These resources are especially notable for connecting music to social studies through interdisciplinary study. Lesson plans include suggested grade levels and the time necessary to complete the various activities. They focus mostly on music from the 1960s and 1970s (although music from other eras is represented, too), and lists of relevant songs with artist and recording information are provided for each. African American music is explored in detail, and emphasis is placed on viewing music as a form of narrative poetry and as social force.

LESSON
PLANNING
RESOURCES
FOREIGN LANGUAGES

WORLD WIDE ARTS RESOURCES
HTTP://WWAR.COM

World Wide Arts Resources is a gateway to contemporary visual and performing arts news, art blogs, art history, contemporary artists, and gallery portfolios. Artwork can be searched by artist, media, theme, country of origin, date, and price. This website offers an extensive art history section with summaries of different movements and biographies of the masters. Emphasis is placed on multicultural art, and educators can browse artists based on nationality. Information is also available regarding museums and galleries as well as current art news.

FOREIGN LANGUAGES

AMERICAN ASSOCIATION OF TEACHERS OF FRENCH
HTTP://WWW.FRENCHTEACHERS.ORG

The American Association of Teachers of French provides classroom activities, many of which include audiovisual resources. Advocacy tools that target increasing enrollment and promoting French language study are also available, and educators can find an archive of newsletters with helpful articles related to teaching French.

AMERICAN ASSOCIATION OF TEACHERS OF GERMAN
HTTP://WWW.AATG.ORG

The American Association of Teachers of German emphasizes the use of web technology in teaching German. Multimedia resources, such as radio, magazines, and newspapers, are stressed. The GROW (German Resources on the Web) section, located under Teaching Resources, has a wealth of information and classroom resources that are organized according to grammatical content and theme. The variety of German dialects is also stressed through resources that showcase how the German language is used in Austria, Liechtenstein, and Switzerland.

ASIA SOCIETY
HTTP://ASIASOCIETY.ORG/EDUCATION-
LEARNING/RESOURCES-SCHOOLS

Asia Society offers teaching resources for the study of Asian languages and cultures in a K–12 setting. Thematic lesson plans emphasize the history, culture, and diversity of Asia. Assessment tools and professional development opportunities are available. Resources are also available on how to incorporate web-based tools into a curriculum.

CLASSICAL LANGUAGE INSTRUCTION PROJECT
HTTP://WWW.PRINCETON.EDU/~CLIP

The Classical Language Instruction Project (CLIP) aims to improve students' listening and reading skills in Greek and Latin. This website hosts text samples of both prose and poetry along with accompanying audio clips. There is also a section that explains Greek and Latin rhythm, meter, and scansion.

E. L. EASTON
HTTP://ELEASTON.COM

E. L. Easton provides resources on foreign language education. This website serves as a bibliography of online information to aid with the study of Albanian, Arabic, Chinese, Croatian, English, French, German, Hebrew, Italian, Japanese, Latin, Polish, Russian, and Spanish. Links to sample activities and quizzes are provided, along with information on teaching methods. In addition to these free resources, a list of links to bookstores can help readers keep track of foreign language titles available from around the world.

EAST ASIAN STUDIES CENTER
HTTP://WWW.INDIANA.EDU/~EASC/
OUTREACH/EDUCATORS/INDEX.SHTML

The East Asian Studies Center at Indiana University offers resources for educators focusing on China, Japan, Taiwan, and Korea. Thematic units and lesson plans, such as one on Japanese monsters, offer cultural information in addition to language study. Workshops are available for

K–12 teachers and audio and video resources are available as well as standards and proficiency information.

FLTEACH FORUM

HTTP://WWW.CORTLAND.EDU/FLTEACH

FLTeach: Foreign Language Teaching Forum hosts a database of lesson planning resources, with a particularly strong library of French and Spanish materials. Resources are easy to search by topic, keyword, language, skill, grade level, and standard. The material on this website can serve as a starting point for original lesson plans, but there are also some links to premade lesson plans, if you should want to use them. Educators can also subscribe to the FLTEACH listserv to receive updates and participate in discussions.

GOETHE INSTITUTE

HTTP://WWW.GOETHE.DE/ENINDEX.HTM

The Goethe Institute offers a number of German language resources. In the Teacher Service section, educators can find cultural information and materials as well as a subsection on German for early learners. In the Learner Projects section of the Materials tab, there are activities and games for students, including an international e-mail project that connects German-speaking students from around the world. A free newsletter is also available for educators.

ILOVELANGUAGES

HTTP://WWW.ILOVELANGUAGES.COM

iLoveLanguages is a catalog of language-related Internet resources including language lessons, translating dictionaries, native literature, translation services, software, and links to language schools. Of the more than 200 languages listed, 76 offer lesson plans and curriculum resources. This website also includes job listings as well as student camps and programs. (Do note, however, that this is a rather old website, and some of the links no longer function.)

LANGUAGE LINKS

HTTP://WWW.LANGLINK.NET/LANGLINK

This website offers annotated links to websites for language teachers and language learners. Of particular interest are links to web-based teaching activities arranged by language. Curriculum resources for African languages, Asian languages, English as a Second Language (ESL), French, German, Italian, and Russian are available, among others, as are links to websites providing cultural information—often in foreign languages—for countries from around the world.

LANGUAGES ONLINE (AU)

HTTP://WWW.EDUCATION.VIC.GOV.AU/LANGUAGESONLINE/

Languages Online (AU) offers an array of online and print resources for educators. Thematic packets are available in addition to audio aids and songs. The languages offered include Chinese, French, German, Indonesian, Italian, Macedonian, Spanish, and Turkish. This website also offers assessment and progress tracking tools.

LANGUAGES ONLINE (UK)

HTTP://ATSCHOOL.EDUWEB.CO.UK/RGSHIWYC/
SCHOOL/CURRIC/HOTPOTATOES/INDEX.HTM

Languages Online (UK) focuses on French, German, Italian, Latin, and Spanish. Online activities and games are available as well as some audio resources. This website also includes a listing of accent codes and typing tools for all five covered languages. In addition to resources for educators, this website includes many links for students.

LANGSOURCE: REVIEWS OF LANGUAGE & CULTURAL RESOURCES

HTTP://WWW.LANGSOURCE.UMD.EDU

LangSource offers an annotated listing of teaching materials both print and multimedia as well as reviews of these materials. This collection is useful for the study of Arabic, Chinese, German, Hausa, Hindi, Japanese, Korean, Quechua, Spanish, Tamil, and Yoruba. Educators can search for resources according to type, category, grade level, topic, and national standard. This website also includes links to related online resources.

LIFE IN NEW CHINA

HTTP://WWW.WHATKIDSCANDO.ORG/
CHINA_SITE/INDEX.HTML

Life in New China is a photo essay project completed by students in Beijing. With this website, participating students aimed to increase international understanding of the culture and diversity of their city. Resources include a dictionary slideshow and photographs taken throughout Beijing. This website also offers links to other resources.

MISCOSITAS

HTTP://WWW.MISCOSITAS.COM

MisCositas offers lesson plans organized into thematic units in English, Spanish, French, and Chinese. Emphasis is placed on the customs and beliefs of different cultures, and resources include songs and coloring sheets. This website is particularly helpful for providing program building resources, and one section explains how web-based teaching tools can be incorporated into foreign language curricula. Educational videos and links to outside videos are also available.

MULTILINGUAL BOOKS

HTTP://WWW.MULTILINGUALBOOKS.COM/MBCONTENT.HTML

Multilingual Books offers an array of foreign language resources. This site provides links to newspapers from around the world and to online dictionaries, including ones that specialize in medical and technical language and foreign slang. Search-friendly Internet radio is also available in a number of different languages. The site also hosts links to free language lessons in more than 20 different languages.

PANWAPA

HTTP://WWW.PANWAPA.COM

Panwapa is a K–2 curriculum created by the people behind *Sesame Street*. This curriculum aims to highlight the similarities and differences within the global community in the hopes of increasing students' understanding of world diversity. Its multidisciplinary approach includes social studies, math, language arts, science, and health. Information is available in Arabic, English, Japanese, Mandarin, and Spanish.

SUSSEX CENTRE FOR LANGUAGE STUDIES

HTTP://WWW.SUSSEX.AC.UK/LANGUAGES

The Sussex Centre for Language Studies at the University of Sussex offers an annotated bibliography of online resources. Chinese, English, French, German, Italian, Japanese, Russian, and Spanish constitute the bulk of these resources, but a section is devoted to lesser known world languages. This website offers a wide range of resources regarding the news and media from around the world. Links to teaching resources are plentiful, and there is some attention paid to culture and heritage.

UCLA LANGUAGE MATERIALS PROJECT

HTTP://WWW.LMP.UCLA.EDU

The goal of the UCLA Language Materials Project is to increase literacy in less commonly taught languages, and information is available regarding the countries and regions associated with them. Many of the lesson plans offered here, however, could be adapted to fit any language. Resources can be searched by language, material, level, and audience (grade level). A listing of both print and online resources is available.

SCIENCE, TECHNOLOGY, ENGINEERING, AND MATH (STEM)

AMERICAN ASSOCIATION FOR THE ADVANCEMENT OF SCIENCE: PROJECT 2061

HTTP://WWW.PROJECT2061.ORG

Project 2061 is an initiative of the American Association for the Advancement of Science (AAAS) aimed at increasing literacy in science, mathematics, and technology. In order to reform K–12 science education nationwide, this initiative has produced curriculum resources and professional development opportunities. Textbook evaluations are available as well as resources for parents and caregivers.

BILL NYE

HTTP://WWW.BILLNYE.COM/FOR-KIDS-TEACHERS

This website is managed by Bill Nye "The Science Guy." Educators can find demonstrations and experiments for interactive hands-on learning. Episode guides are also available to complement Bill Nye's educational television show. This website offers resources that cover a number of mathematics and science topics.

CUT THE KNOT

HTTP://WWW.CUT-THE-KNOT.ORG

Cut the Knot is a website devoted to mathematics education. Emphasis is placed on the importance of visual aids and active participation in math. This website boasts hundreds of interactive math demos, activities, games, and puzzles. These resources are arranged by subject and cover a wide range of topics, from arithmetic and algebra to combinatorics, fractals, and chaos theory.

DISCOVERY EDUCATION

HTTP://SCHOOL.DISCOVERYEDUCATION.COM/INDEX.HTML

Discovery Education offers lesson plans for K–12 teachers in traditional subject areas, such as history, mathematics, and science. This website also offers educators a customizable puzzle maker for crosswords, word searches, and other puzzles. The science, technology, engineering, and mathematics (STEM) resources here are particularly useful.

EPA TEACHER RESOURCES

HTTP://WWW.EPA.GOV/STUDENTS/TEACHERS.HTML

The Environmental Protection Agency (EPA) offers information and lesson planning resources organized according to topic and grade level. The oil spill education resources are especially notable. The website also offers information regarding community service projects that can easily be incorporated into a service-learning curriculum. Grants and funding opportunities for K–12 classrooms can be found as well.

EXPLORELEARNING'S GIZMOS™

HTTP://WWW.EXPLOREMATH.COM

ExploreLearning's Gizmos™ are online simulations for grades 3–12 that "power inquiry and understanding." These instructional tools cover a variety of areas in math and science, including probability, the greenhouse effect, and rollercoaster physics. Resources can be browsed by subject and grade level along with academic standard or textbook. Professional development and training is available for educators wanting to incorporate the Gizmos into their curricula. A 30-day free trial is available and provides access to a library of more than 450 Gizmos.

EXPLORING THE ENVIRONMENT™ THROUGH GLOBAL CLIMATE CHANGE EDUCATION

HTTP://ETE.CET.EDU/MODULES/MODULES.HTML

Exploring the Environment through Global Climate Change Education (ETE-GCC) is run by The Center for Educational Technologies at Wheeling Jesuit University with funding from the NASA Innovations in Global Climate Change Education program. The site offers problem-based learning (PBL) modules that aim to increase climate literacy among students. The basic questions asked by the PBL model are

"What do we know?", "What do we need to know?", and "What should we do?" By answering these questions, students are expected to generate unique solutions to current environmental issues. Proponents of the model argue that by actively learning the material, students achieve greater metacognition and can better retain knowledge. This site gives a useful overview of the theory and structure of PBL along with several science modules. Notes are also available on how to assess learning in the PBL model.

HANDS-ON EQUATIONS

HTTP://WWW.BORENSON.COM

Hands-On Equations is a supplementary program that incorporates sight and touch into the math curriculum to help introduce algebraic concepts to students in grades 3–8. Students use hands-on visual representations of problems, setting up equations as game pieces, and then play algebra as a game in order to solve the equation. Developed by Dr. Henry Borenson, this teaching system enables young children to understand and solve algebraic equations, improving their self-esteem and interest in mathematics. Homeschooling resources are also available.

ILLUMINATIONS

HTTP://ILLUMINATIONS.NCTM.ORG

Illuminations, hosted by the National Council of Teachers of Mathematics, is a database of lesson plans accompanied by applets, simulations, and manipulatives that can be used in math classrooms. Everything is easily searchable and organized according to grade level and, for lesson plans, topic. Topics include number and operations, algebra, geometry, measurement, and data analysis and probability. These simulations and manipulatives are designed for students in grades pre-K–12.

LET'S TALK SCIENCE
HTTP://WWW.LETSTALKSCIENCE.CA/EDUCATORS

Let's Talk Science is a Canadian website dedicated to outreach and improving science education. Early learning and hands-on activities are stressed. Lesson planning resources are organized by category and provide information on target age, setting, and time needed. This organization also hosts the All Science Challenge for Canadian students in grades 6–8. This competition challenges teams of four in a series of question/answer competitions as well as in hands-on design challenges.

MATHEMATICS EDUCATION AT NORTHERN KENTUCKY UNIVERSITY
HTTP://WWW.NKU.EDU/~MATHED/GIFTED.HTML

The mathematics education department at Northern Kentucky University houses an extensive list of resources for parents and teachers of students who show promise in mathematics. Educators can find links to problems, resources, and games for students in addition to textbook and curriculum resources. Grade-level competency charts are also available. Sample lesson plans can be found for grades 5–8 in algebra, probability, and geometry. This site also includes links to virtual manipulatives that can be used for classroom demonstration.

THE MATH FORUM
HTTP://WWW.MATHFORUM.ORG

The Math Forum is an online resource made available by Drexel University. Professional development opportunities, community discussions, and a newsletter are offered for educators. In the Ask Dr. Math section, elementary to college students can find an extensive list of formulas, problem sets and answers, and other recommended math sites. This site also lists camps and summer programs for students as well as activities, problems, and games. The Teacher2Teacher section hosts other planning resources, and the Quick Reference link gives educators access to problems of the week in different topics. Also accessible from the Quick Reference page is Math Tools, a community library of technology-based tools, lessons, activities, and support materials for teaching and learning mathematics. Specific information relates to the use of calculators, computers, and mobile devices.

MINERAL INFORMATION INSTITUTE
HTTP://WWW.MII.ORG/LESSONS.HTML

The Mineral Information Institute offers a number of lesson plan starters that focus on the study of minerals. These resources target primary and elementary school students and seek to integrate physical science with other subjects through the study of minerals. This website hosts a number of helpful starting points that allow educators to build their own lesson plans.

NASA EDUCATION
HTTP://WWW.NASA.GOV/AUDIENCE/
FOREDUCATORS/INDEX.HTML

The NASA Education website is geared to science educators. This website is easy to search, with resources organized according to grade level, subject, topic, and resource type. NASA Television offers educational programming available to stream and educational podcasts are available as well. There are also resources on how to make original podcasts using audio and video clips from NASA. Professional development is available through NASA Educator Resource Centers nationwide.

NATIONAL COUNCIL OF TEACHERS OF MATHEMATICS
HTTP://NCTM.ORG

The National Council of Teachers of Mathematics is a public voice of mathematics education that supports teachers and works to ensure equitable and high-quality mathematics instruction for all students. The website includes teaching standards, conference information, and publications. The Curriculum Focal Points for students in pre-K–grade 8 target specific math skills and topics in order to ensure students' continued success. The Focus in High School Mathematics framework serves to bolster reasoning and critical thinking skills. Educators can find example problems, lessons plans, and other helpful resources on this site. Parents and families can also find resources to help their students achieve success in math.

NATIONAL LIBRARY OF VIRTUAL MANIPULATIVES
HTTP://NLVM.USU.EDU/EN/NAV/VLIBRARY.HTML

The National Library of Virtual Manipulatives is a database of applets, simulations, and manipulations that can supplement K–12 math lessons. These resources are organized according to five categories: algebra, data analysis and probability, geometry, measurement, and number and operations. This website offers useful visual aids to supplement any standard math curriculum.

NOAA NATIONAL OCEAN SERVICE EDUCATION
HTTP://OCEANSERVICE.NOAA.GOV/
EDUCATION/LESSONS/WELCOME.HTML

The National Oceanic and Atmospheric Administration (NOAA) National Ocean Service Education website hosts a number of lesson plans that aim to increase ocean and climate literacy among K–12 students. These lesson plans are organized topically and relate to chemistry, Earth science, geography, life science, math, and physical science curricula. Under the Curriculum section of the Teachers tab, curricula can be found for students in grades 6–12 focusing on estuaries, remote sensing, and ocean exploration. This website also offers interactive simulations for students, tutorials, games, and hands-on projects.

PROJECT M²: MENTORING YOUNG MATHEMATICIANS
HTTP://WEB2.UCONN.EDU/PROJECTM2

Project M^2 is a curriculum and research study that focuses on geometry and measurement skills in kindergarten and first and second grades. Project M^2 incorporates an interdisciplinary framework by combining math lessons with children's literature and reading as well as lessons about animals. Although this curriculum is still being field tested, the number of activities provided for use both in and outside the classroom is promising.

PROJECT M³: MENTORING MATHEMATICAL MINDS

HTTP://WWW.GIFTED.UCONN.EDU/PROJECTM3/INDEX.HTML

Project M³ targets math skills for students in grades 3–5. In each grade, four units are emphasized: algebraic thinking, data analysis and probability, number skills, and geometry and measurement. Students are encouraged to keep a "Mathematician's Journal" that teaches them "how to think, write, and act like mathematicians to solve the problem." Home activities are available to supplement classroom lessons. Books, articles, and online resources for educators are also available.

SCIENCE NETLINKS

HTTP://WWW.SCIENCENETLINKS.COM/MATRIX.PHP

Science NetLinks hosts a database of K–12 lesson plans in a wide range of sciences. These lessons include hands-on demonstrations and experiments in addition to interactive online student activities. Curriculum standards and benchmarks are easily explained, and educators can also find a number of printable worksheets and student e-sheets.

SEA SEMESTER

HTTP://WWW.SEA.EDU/ACADEMICS/K12.ASPX

SEA Semester's website offers K–12 lesson plans that center on marine biology, oceanography, and nautical science. Student activities and extension projects are strongly encouraged in order to promote independent study. Evaluation and assessment tools are available. SEA Semester also hosts summer programs in oceanography for high school students.

SCIENCE AND MATHEMATICS INITIATIVE FOR LEARNING ENHANCEMENT

HTTP://MYPAGES.IIT.EDU/~SMILE/INDEX.HTML

The Science and Mathematics Initiative for Learning Enhancement (SMILE) offers almost 900 free lesson plans for elementary, middle, and high school educators. Educators can find lesson plans for biology, chemistry, physics, and math classrooms. This website also includes links to outside resources.

SERVICE LEARNING

CONSTITUTIONAL RIGHTS FOUNDATION
HTTP://WWW.CRF-USA.ORG

The Constitutional Rights Foundation (CRF) aims to teach students the meaning of citizenship through service learning. The CRF works with museums and libraries to enhance students' understanding of law, government, and civic participation. Online lesson plans are available, covering topics such as American history, immigration, intellectual property, and school violence. This organization also sponsors a mock trial program for students and hosts links to various publications and other resources.

FACING THE FUTURE
HTTP://WWW.FACINGTHEFUTURE.ORG

Facing the Future is an organization aimed at supporting youth action in local communities. This site hosts a step-by-step guide to implementing a service-learning project. Educators can find a database of service-learning project ideas that focus on global or national issues as well as specific projects targeting the state of Washington. The ideas in the Climate Change Action Projects section are particularly noteworthy, targeting environmental science and energy sustainability. Grade-level information and links to related online materials are available. Curriculum resources on global issues and sustainability are also available, and some chapters of textbooks can be accessed for free. Information concerning ongoing research and funding is presented, and a bibliography of journals, studies, newsletters, and listservs related to service learning is also available.

GOTOSERVICELEARNING

HTTP://WWW.GOTOSERVICELEARNING.ORG

Created in part by the Youth Service America and America's Promise Alliance organizations, GoToServiceLearning is a database of lesson plans that incorporate service-learning themes into traditional subject areas. Lesson plans can be easily searched by subject, service-learning theme, grade level (K–3, 4–6, 6–8, and 9–12), duration, setting (suburban, rural, and urban), and place of impact, including local, national, global, and virtual communities. This database also offers lesson plans for students with special needs and for youth at risk of dropping out.

KIDS CONSORTIUM

HTTP://WWW.KIDSCONSORTIUM.ORG

KIDS Consortium offers service-learning resources for K–12 students in Maine and the rest of New England. This organization stresses three key principles: academic integrity, apprentice citizenship, and student ownership. In these projects, students make important decisions with their adult sponsors, each of whom acts as a partner and coach. Workshops are offered for educators and the community. Projects that involve history, ecology, or STEM-related fields are especially encouraged. Mini-grants are available for beginning and sustaining a service-learning curriculum.

LEARNING TO GIVE

HTTP://LEARNINGTOGIVE.ORG

Learning to Give is an organization that focuses on teaching students the importance of philanthropy and character building by "giving their time and talent to the community." This website offers more than 1,600 K–12 lessons plans organized by grade level, keyword, subject, and educational standard. A children's literature guide is available as well as numerous links to student activities. Educators can find resources on African American, Japanese, Jewish, Korean, and women's philanthropy in order to encourage greater understanding of diversity in the classroom. There is also a section for parents.

NATIONAL SERVICE-LEARNING CLEARINGHOUSE
HTTP://WWW.SERVICELEARNING.ORG

The National Service-Learning Clearinghouse (NSLC) provides information and resources to support service learning in the classroom. Educators can browse the Service-Learning Ideas and Curricular Examples (SLICE) database, locate funding opportunities for service-learning projects, and download guides such as the *K–12 Service-Learning Project Planning Toolkit, High Quality Instruction That Transforms: A Guide to Implementing Quality Academic Service-Learning,* and *Service-Learning in Community-Based Organizations: A Practical Guide to Starting and Sustaining High-Quality Programs.* A sister site, Youth Sharing Ideas & Tools for Engagement (YouthSITE; http://www.servicelearning.org/youthsite), allows students to connect with peers to discuss service learning. This website also includes information on awards, grants, and subgrants, and it offers a free newsletter. In addition, there is a section that provides information and resources for parents.

THE STRAWBERRY POINT SCHOOL
SERVICE LEARNING PRIMER
HTTP://GOODCHARACTER.COM/SERVICE/PRIMER-1.HTML

The Strawberry Point School's service-learning program offers students the chance to reach academic goals through involvement in community service projects. This model argues that service learning engages and motivates students and makes for authentic learning experiences. The program instructs that service-learning projects be broken into three stages: preparation, action, and reflection. This website offers step-by-step instructions on how to create, implement, and assess service-learning projects. In addition to numerous classroom success stories, this website offers example questions of reflection and assessment tools.

UNITED WE SERVE

HTTP://SERVE.GOV

United We Serve is a website aimed at increasing community service across the U.S. Although many of the resources available here are geared toward adult service projects, a number of them can be incorporated into K–12 classrooms. There are toolkits for creating education, health, energy, and other projects, as well a "Create Your Own" option. The section on community projects to assist veterans and military families is particularly well developed. The Let's Read. Let's Move. initiative promotes healthy lifestyles for students and encourages summer reading in order to prevent learning loss during vacation. The most useful classroom resources are in the 9/11 National Day of Service & Remembrance section, which includes lesson plans and student activities.

YOUTH SERVICE AMERICA

HTTP://WWW.YSA.ORG

Youth Service America (YSA) aims to strengthen the "youth voice" of students ages 5–25. The YSA sponsors Global Youth Service Day in April and runs the Semester of Service program, which offers students the chance to immerse themselves in a long-term service-learning project. Educators can find information on grants to support service learning as well as downloadable resources like *100 Ways to Change the World* and *Effective Practices for Engaging At-Risk Youth in Service.* An e-mail newsletter is also available for subscription. Get Ur Good On (http://www.geturgoodon.org) is an affiliated website where students can upload photos and videos about their service projects and connect with peers also involved in community service. Resources are also available in Spanish.

SOCIAL STUDIES

C-SPAN CLASSROOM

HTTP://WWW.C-SPANCLASSROOM.ORG

C-SPAN Classroom is a video database that can be easily incorporated into civics, government, or history curricula. Videos range from a few minutes to more than an hour in length, and the database is easily searchable by topic and program type. Emphasis is placed on utilizing these videos as debate starters. Free posters, newsletters, and other classroom resources are also available.

CENTER FOR CIVIC EDUCATION

HTTP://NEW.CIVICED.ORG

The Center for Civic Education offers lesson-planning resources for K–12 educators on a variety of topics including Black History Month, voting, and the presidencies of Washington, Madison, and Lincoln. Specific resources are also available regarding Independence Day and Constitution Day. The Project Citizen initiative allows students to directly participate in public policy by determining an issue, developing a solution, and then creating a plan of action in order to have their public policy proposal adopted by the local or state government. The School Violence Prevention Demonstration Program aims to help students better understand concepts of authority, justice, responsibility, and privacy in order to prevent bullying and other forms of school violence.

THE CENTER ON CONGRESS

HTTP://CENTERONCONGRESS.ORG

The Center on Congress at Indiana University aims to increase student understanding of government and citizenship. Educators can find lesson plans, videos, and a section dedicated to teaching with primary sources. Students can also explore interactive modules and a virtual Congress. Emphasis is placed on understanding how representatives make decisions. The center also assists in the production of *TIME for*

Kids, a free mini-magazine for classrooms with grade-appropriate information and activities.

ECEDWEB: ECONOMIC EDUCATION WEB

HTTP://ECEDWEB.UNOMAHA.EDU/LESSONS/LESSONS.CFM

Economic Education Web hosts a number of economics lesson plans for students in grades K–12. Resources from this database are organized according to grade level, content area, and concept. The Teach History and Economics of Nebraska (THEN) initiative for K–6 students offers student activities. Virtual economics companion lessons are also included as well as information regarding national and Nebraska standards.

ECONEDLINK

HTTP://WWW.ECONEDLINK.ORG/EDUCATOR

EconEdLink offers economics and personal finance lesson plans organized by type, concept, standard, grade level, author, and interactive resources. Lesson plans include educator reviews and suggestions for classroom integration. Interactive tools such as a compound interest calculator are also available. Emphasis is placed on connecting lesson plans to current events.

FEDERAL RESERVE EDUCATION

HTTP://WWW.FEDERALRESERVEEDUCATION.ORG

The Federal Reserve sponsors resources for K–12 educators. Lesson plans focus on banking, economics, the Federal Reserve, monetary policy, money, and personal finance. In addition to lesson plans, student activities, online exhibits, and WebQuests are available. A history of the Federal Reserve is presented, and many Federal Reserve publications can be freely accessed. There is also information on the High School Fed Challenge and other academic competitions.

FEEDING MINDS, FIGHTING HUNGER
HTTP://WWW.FEEDINGMINDS.ORG

Feeding Minds, Fighting Hunger is a website focused on teaching K–12 students about hunger, malnutrition, and food insecurity. Lesson plans, student activities, handouts, and WebQuests are available at the primary, intermediate, and secondary levels. The goal of the website is to spur student action through education, and these resources would fit nicely into a larger service-learning project concerning world hunger. One section of the website is devoted to students interested in independent learning.

FOSSILS-FACTS-AND-FINDS.COM
HTTP://WWW.FOSSILS-FACTS-AND-FINDS.COM

Fossils-facts-and-finds.com is a website devoted to teaching students about fossils and the basic principles of geology. This website was founded by two teachers who love "cool rocks" and use the site to promote a greater appreciation for their study. Students can find information on different categories of fossils as well as an explanation and chart of geologic time. Information on how to start a geology club is also included. Educators can find geology lesson plans and activities such as coloring pages, crosswords, and word searches.

FOUNDATION FOR TEACHING ECONOMICS
HTTP://WWW.FTE.ORG

The Foundation for Teaching Economics provides lesson plans that connect economic concepts and standards to current events. Specific lesson plans describe the role of economic forces in American history and the way economics relates to the environment, including a section on the economics of disasters. The Economics for Leaders lesson plans are notable for their free downloadable PowerPoint presentations, which complement student activities. There is also a section specifically designed for educators who are teaching economics for the first time.

THE GILDER LEHRMAN INSTITUTE
OF AMERICAN HISTORY

HTTP://WWW.GILDERLEHRMAN.ORG

The Gilder Lehrman Institute of American History offers videos, booklists, podcasts, and curriculum modules on material spanning from the founding of the U.S. to the present. The Gilder Lehrman Collection, meanwhile, boasts 60,000 primary source documents available for search, including letters, diaries, maps, pamphlets, and other ephemera. The sections regarding Abraham Lincoln, slavery, and abolition are particularly strong. Students can explore online exhibitions as well as compete in essay contests and scholarship competitions. This organization also offers traveling exhibits and Saturday classes at select schools nationwide. Links to related online resources are provided.

HISTORICAL THINKING MATTERS

HTTP://HISTORICALTHINKINGMATTERS.ORG

Historical Thinking Matters is a site dedicated to presenting history to students in a fun and exciting way. Students are taught to view historians as detectives investigating the past and emphasis is placed on how to "critique and construct historical narratives." Primary sources such as journals, maps, photographs, advertisements, and sheet music are available for use as well as essay topics, discussion questions, and WebQuests. Topics include the Spanish-American War, the Scopes Trial, Social Security, and Rosa Parks.

LIBRARY OF CONGRESS

HTTP://WWW.LOC.GOV/TEACHERS

The Library of Congress works to foster inquiry into primary sources by students and educators. In order to achieve this goal, original documents and other resources are made available online. Lesson plans including primary source materials are arranged according to topic and era, with information on appropriate grade levels provided. There are also links to a timeline of U.S. history, classroom activities, presentations, and games.

THE LIVING ROOM CANDIDATE

HTTP://WWW.LIVINGROOMCANDIDATE.ORG

The Living Room Candidate is a database of presidential campaign commercials from 1952 to 2012. In addition to analysis of both major candidates' advertising campaigns, educators can also find maps of corresponding election results. The Admaker online video editing tool challenges students to transform historical commercials for one candidate into a commercial for the opponent. Lesson plans on this website emphasize critical analysis and increased understanding of political language. Resources are organized according to year, issue, and type of commercial.

NATIONAL ARCHIVES

HTTP://ARCHIVES.GOV/EDUCATION

The National Archives offers primary sources and other resources, including video conferences and activities. Lesson plans are available covering U.S. history from 1754 to the present, and an 8-day summer workshop is offered for educators interested in learning about how to incorporate primary sources into the classroom. This website focuses on "History in the Raw," which means presenting students with primary historical documents and allowing them to synthesize original ideas regarding the subject. Regional education information is presented along with information on national standards of education for civics, history, and government.

THE NATIONAL ARCHIVES (UK)

HTTP://WWW.NATIONALARCHIVES.GOV.UK/EDUCATION

The UK's National Archives offers a wealth of primary source material and lesson planning resources on the history of the United Kingdom. This archive focuses on material from the medieval era to the present. In addition to traditional classroom materials, this website also hosts podcasts and a virtual classroom to facilitate discussion of historical interpretations.

NATIONAL COUNCIL FOR THE SOCIAL STUDIES

HTTP://WWW.SOCIALSTUDIES.ORG

The National Council for the Social Studies aims to ensure that students have an adequate understanding of the past so that they can become informed citizens of the 21st century. This organization offers conferences and workshops as well as information regarding state and regional councils. Advocacy tools are also available. Educators can find professional curriculum standards and lesson plans. This website notably offers resources for teaching about current events, Iraq, and 9/11 for civics, history, geography, government, or economics classes.

NATIONAL GEOGRAPHIC EDUCATION

HTTP://EDUCATION.NATIONALGEOGRAPHIC.COM

National Geographic Education offers student activities and lesson plans that cover numerous science, social studies, and geography topics. Lesson are available for grades K–12 and are connected to national standards. A mapping tool and links to educational videos serve to promote geo-literacy in the classroom. A free monthly newsletter is also available.

SMITHSONIAN SOURCE

HTTP://WWW.SMITHSONIANSOURCE.ORG

Smithsonian Source provides educators with five different methods of teaching with primary sources in K–12 classrooms: Artifact & Document Analysis, Compare & Contrast, Four Corners/Jig Saw, Graphic Organizers, and the PERSIA (Political, Economic, Religious, Social, Intellectual, Artistic) approach. Each method includes lesson plans, video, primary sources, and Document Based Questions (DBQs). The collection of primary sources includes artifacts, documents, and photographs, organized thematically. Topics include westward expansion, transportation, civil rights, invention, colonial America, and Native American history.

THE STOCK MARKET GAME™

HTTP://WWW.STOCKMARKETGAME.ORG

The Stock Market Game can be used with students in grades 4–12. In this game, students begin with $100,000 in their virtual cash accounts. They then work in teams to make wise investments and maximize profits. Leadership, cooperation, and negotiation are stressed as students participate in live trading simulations that mirror real-life stock exchanges such as the NASDAQ and the NYSE. Assessment and evaluation tools are available for educators as well as a newsletter. Fees vary from state to state, but the program is available for free in some areas.

TEACHING WITH PRIMARY SOURCES

HTTP://WWW.LOC.GOV/TEACHERS/TPS

In collaboration with educational organizations, Teaching with Primary Sources (TPS) delivers professional development programs to help teachers access Library of Congress resources for use in K–12 classrooms. A consortium member list is available, and many regional areas have their own TPS websites with information on local workshops and further resources. Educators can also download the latest issue of *The Teaching with Primary Sources Journal* from this site.

WASHINGTON STATE HISTORICAL SOCIETY

HTTP://STORIES.WASHINGTONHISTORY.ORG/
EDUCATION/TEACHERS/INDEX.SHTML

The Washington State Historical Society offers lesson planning resources for grades 3–12. Resources are organized according to theme; topics include Native American history, westward expansion, transportation, environmental history, the civil rights movement, and the women's rights movement. Both primary and secondary source material is included in each lesson plan, and emphasis is placed on understanding historical maps. Links to related online resources are also available.

INDEPENDENT STUDY

CHOOSEMYPLATE.GOV

HTTP://WWW.CHOOSEMYPLATE.GOV

This website is maintained by the U.S. Department of Agriculture and it focuses on health and nutrition education. In addition to an explanation of MyPlate, students can find out valuable information about meal planning and ways to incorporate exercise into their daily routine. Children can play games such as Blast Off in order to learn the importance of daily decision making in overall health. This website also offers classroom materials as well as tips on how to eat healthier.

COOL MATH

HTTP://WWW.COOLMATH.COM

Cool Math is a self-described "amusement park of math and more" created with the goal of making math fun. It can help students who are having trouble with math, but it is also designed to address the needs of students who are bored in math class and want to learn more. Arithmetic lessons are numerous, but the material ranges from basic addition and subtraction to introductory material on fractals and limits. Along with games and activities, this website offers a math survival guide for students who feel discouraged in mathematics.

COOL SCIENCE FOR CURIOUS KIDS

HTTP://WWW.HHMI.ORG/COOLSCIENCE/FORKIDS

Cool Science for Curious Kids offers students a chance to study the basics of plant and animal science. In addition to learning about butterfly metamorphosis and the various parts of a plant, students can complete the 1" Square Project. This project helps students study nature without a microscope by looking at their environment through a 1" window. Students are encouraged to look at a variety of natural elements, including tree trunks, leaves, flowers, and soil. A worksheet is also available so that students can record their observations, and emphasis is placed on the way that scientists use observation in order to study nature.

DINOSAURS FOR KIDS
HTTP://WWW.KIDSDINOS.COM

At Dinosaurs for Kids, students can study paleontology at their own pace. Activities help students learn how to categorize different dinosaurs and then how to place them on the geologic timeline. There is also a map for students interested in learning about which dinosaurs came from where and how climate impacted their existences. Students can play a number of educational dinosaur-themed games as well as vote for their favorite dinosaur in various polls.

FACT MONSTER™
HTTP://WWW.FACTMONSTER.COM

Fact Monster™ is an online almanac, dictionary, and encyclopedia that includes many student-friendly games, quizzes, and activities. The Homework Center can help students study geography, history, language arts, science, and social studies, and it also provides help with writing, speaking, and basic studying skills. In addition to the traditional school subjects, students can find information about art and architecture, business and the stock market, fashion, and the history of toys and games. The website's sports section includes histories of sports, records, and fun facts.

FIGURE THIS!
HTTP://FIGURETHIS.ORG

Figure This! is an initiative by the National Council of Teachers of Mathematics that stresses the importance of parental involvement in a student's mathematics education. This website offers a series of math challenges that engage the entire family in solving word problems and

INDEPENDENT STUDY

math modeling problems. In this way, math leaves the classroom and becomes an engaging part of students' everyday lives.

GEONET
HTTP://WWW.EDUPLACE.COM/GEONET

GeoNet allows students to learn about world geography through a series of quizzes and games. Students can choose to find out more about the spatial information, climate, physical geography, population, culture, and ecosystems of each continent. There are two levels of difficulty to choose from. After learning about the world, students can become a GeoChampion!

GIRLSTART
HTTP://WWW.GIRLSTART.ORG

Girlstart is an initiative that encourages girls and young women to be active in the fields of science, technology, engineering, and mathematics (STEM). This website offers girls self-guided lesson plans, most notably in computer science and web design as well as homework help and a list of fun science experiments. A listing of programs, summer camps, and workshops are also offered on this site. Girls can learn basic information about preparing for a college major in the STEM fields and about career information for after college. This website also offers an extensive section on how math and science relate to sports and the importance of female involvement in both of these areas.

INTERNATIONAL CHILDREN'S DIGITAL LIBRARY
HTTP://EN.CHILDRENSLIBRARY.ORG

The International Children's Digital Library makes more than 4,000 children's books available in full-text online. These books range in date from the late 19th century to the present. By offering books in more than 50 languages, this website aims to teach children respect and tolerance of various cultures. Another goal of this library is to contribute to the global community, specifically the shared experiences of children across the world.

INDEPENDENT STUDY

I WAS WONDERING

HTTP://WWW.IWASWONDERING.ORG

I Was Wondering is a project of the National Academy of Sciences that specifically targets girls and young women interested in science. It showcases the accomplishments of historic women in science, while also offering information on contemporary women in science. This website highlights the varied and intriguing careers of some of today's most prominent scientists. Students can write to real scientists with questions and play engaging and creative games related to scientific endeavors.

KIDS ONLINE RESOURCES

HTTP://KIDSOLR.COM

Kids Online Resources (KidsOLR) is an archive of educational links for students and parents. This site includes numerous resources in traditional subject areas such as art, music, geography, history, language arts, math, science, and health. Other topics discussed include home-schooling, Internet safety, entertainment, and games. The Kids of the World section is particularly notable: It provides links to many foreign websites, which, though often not in English, could be helpful for students studying foreign languages or for kids who just want to get a glimpse into the cultures of other countries. There is also a section devoted specifically to teenagers.

IPL2

HTTP://IPL.ORG

ipl2 provides an archive of vetted educational links for children and teens. ipl2 For Kids is especially well put-together, allowing students to browse links by category, such as health & nutrition and sports & recreation, or by traditional subject areas such as history, math, and science. The Reading Zone is particularly notable for its extensive list of resources, as is the Culture Quest, which leads students through an exploration of various cultures. ipl2 For Teens covers topics such as health and sexuality, finances, and graphic novels. Its TeenSpace Poetry and Answers to Frequently Asked Embarrassing Questions (FAEQs) sections are particularly noteworthy. Parent and teacher resources are also available.

MACTUTOR HISTORY OF MATHEMATICS ARCHIVE
HTTP://TURNBULL.MCS.ST-AND.AC.UK/~HISTORY

The MacTutor History of Mathematics archive contains a wide array of primary and secondary materials for the math enthusiast. Biographical information of significant mathematicians is presented by name and date. Theories are arranged by topic and culture of origin, and a history of "famous curves" is included. This online archive also has a section specifically dedicated to female mathematicians.

MATHSCHALLENGE
HTTP://MATHSCHALLENGE.NET

This website was created in response to a variety of popular questions that people have asked about math, such as "Is it impossible to trisect an angle?" and "How do you prove the Pythagorean Theorem?" Students can browse through this list of questions and answers that will challenge them to think beyond the math they are learning in the classroom.

MISSION: CRITICAL
HTTP://WWW.SJSU.EDU/DEPTS/ITL/

Mission: Critical is an interactive tutorial for critical thinking. Students use essential tools of intellectual analysis and are reinforced for successfully completing a series of increasingly complex exercises. Emphasis is placed on the importance of logic.

NICK'S MATHEMATICAL PUZZLES
HTTP://WWW.QBYTE.ORG/PUZZLES

Nick's Mathematical Puzzles is a collection of math puzzles for students, educators, and general math enthusiasts. This website boasts more than 150 puzzles and offers easily understood explanations of each puzzle. The puzzles cover topics such as geometry, probability, number theory, algebra, calculus, trigonometry, and logic, and are rated according to difficulty.

OLOGY

HTTP://WWW.AMNH.ORG/EXPLORE/OLOGY

OLogy is an interactive website offered by the American Museum of Natural History. Students can choose whichever "ology" they wish to learn about and find a variety of educational games and activites related to the topic. They can then proceed through expeditions into various museum exhibits. Subject areas and topics include paleontology, Einstein, astronomy, archaeology, Earth science, and biodiversity, among others.

SCIENCE KIDS

HTTP://WWW.SCIENCEKIDS.CO.NZ

Science Kids is an interactive website that helps students expand upon their interests in science, medicine, and technology. Students can find games, quizzes, and activities as well as science experiments, projects, and independent lesson plans. Topics include animal and plant science, chemistry, light, sound, space, technology, and weather.

TRYSCIENCE

HTTP://WWW.TRYSCIENCE.ORG

At TryScience, students can find a listing of fun science experiments and activities. These activities are posted by various science centers and museums worldwide. The Live Cams section provides a glimpse into some of the different science and technology centers from around the world. By connecting students to these organizations, this website aims to increase student interest in science and foster greater awareness of these institutions.

INDEPENDENT STUDY

JUST FOR FUN

BRAIN BOOSTERS

HTTP://SCHOOL.DISCOVERYEDUCATION.
COM/BRAINBOOSTERS

Brain Boosters is a large, categorized archive of diverse and challenging logic puzzles. These could be incorporated into a curriculum or done just for fun. These puzzles emphasize number skills as well as lateral thinking and spatial awareness.

CARNEGIE LIBRARY OF PITTSBURGH

HTTP://WWW.CARNEGIELIBRARY.ORG/KIDS

This site includes lots of fun reading games and activities for students and is broken into different sections for "big kids" and "little kids." Extensive booklists are available, covering material in a variety of fields. The Homework Help section allows students to target specific subject areas. This site also includes a section on Internet safety.

EDUGAMES

HTTP://WWW.EDUPLACE.COM/EDUGAMES.HTML

EduGames is a Houghton Mifflin website that includes six challenging and educational activities for students. The games listed on this site are particularly helpful for studying language arts. Students can improve their vocabulary as well as their spelling and proofreading skills through these fun, interactive games.

FUNBRAIN

HTTP://WWW.FUNBRAIN.COM/KIDSCENTER.HTML

Funbrain is an educational website that offers a variety of games for students. In addition to recommended readings and madlibs, this site includes a collection of math-based skill games, located in the Math Arcade section. These games can help students improve their arithmetic skills as well as introduce them to basic principles of algebra.

HOWSTUFFWORKS

HTTP://WWW.HOWSTUFFWORKS.COM

HowStuffWorks offers a rich collection of trivia for inquiring minds. Students can find answers to questions in traditional school subject areas and a host of other fields. This site is particularly helpful for information related to science, technology, engineering, and mathematics (STEM). There are also informative blogs, including Stuff to Blow Your Mind, Stuff You Missed in History Class, and The Coolest Stuff on the Planet.

KABOOSE FUNSCHOOL

HTTP://FUNSCHOOL.KABOOSE.COM/INDEX.HTML

Kaboose Funschool offers lots of fun educational games for elementary school students. The Time Warp section offers history games, the Globe Rider section includes geography games, and Formula Fusion focuses on math and science. Students can also find puzzles and coloring sheets as well as a fantastic arts and crafts search engine. The material on this site is aimed at students in grades K–6, and there is a special section for preschoolers as well.

KIDS.GOV

HTTP://KIDS.USA.GOV

Kids.gov is the official kids' portal for the U.S. government. This site links to more than 1,200 webpages from government agencies, schools, and educational organizations, all geared to the various learning levels and interests of kids. In addition to traditional subject areas, this site also offers valuable information regarding health, fitness, safety, money, and personal budgets. Students can also find career resources, as well as information about recreation and the national parks.

KIDSKNOWIT NETWORK

HTTP://WWW.KIDSKNOWIT.COM

The organizers behind the KidsKnowIt Network believe education should be fun and free, with an emphasis on *free*. This website offers

JUST FOR FUN

educational games, movies, music, posters, and other materials at no cost (besides shipping, when applicable). A wide range of topics is covered, including astronomy, biology, math, memory, geology, and more.

KINETIC CITY
HTTP://WWW.KINETICCITY.COM

Kinetic City is a children's website sponsored by the American Association for the Advancement of Science and the National Science Foundation. This science-themed website offers students games, experiments, and activities to explore topics such as biodiversity, human anatomy, and energy. On this site, students are encouraged to play educational games in order to earn points that will save Earth from an alien invasion. This site encourages hands-on learning and offers many interactive learning opportunities.

LEARNING GAMES AT THE KIDZ PAGE
HTTP://WWW.THEKIDZPAGE.COM/
LEARNINGGAMES/INDEX.HTM

The Kidz Page contains a large collection of educational games for students. These include word searches, logic puzzles, and more. Students can target specific skills, such as arithmetic, language arts, and even memory. Some of the games and activities are geared toward students interested in music and the arts.

THE LEARNING NETWORK
HTTP://LEARNING.BLOGS.NYTIMES.COM

With this *New York Times* website, students can stay well informed about the topics that affect them most within the educational system. Topics such as bullying, dress codes, and banned books are placed in the spotlight alongside larger news stories and traditional subjects. Students ages 13 and older are invited to participate in discussions and debates, and quizzes are available for students to test their knowledge of grammar and current affairs. Educators can also find lesson planning resources, most notably Poetry Pairing, which ties a work of poetry to either a photograph or an excerpt from a historical or recent *New York Times* article.

MENSA FOR KIDS

HTTP://WWW.MENSAFORKIDS.ORG

Mensa for Kids is a website sponsored by the high-IQ society Mensa. Here students can find educational games and activities for children and teens. This site's strongest features are its language arts word games, geography activities, and games targeting specific math skills. Parents and educators can also find helpful resources here.

NASA KIDS' CLUB

HTTP://WWW.NASA.GOV/AUDIENCE/FORKIDS/
KIDSCLUB/FLASH/INDEX.HTML

This site offers fun games that allow students to explore and learn about space, build and launch rockets, and explore Mars. Students can also learn about keeping airplanes on schedule and work to help a comet travel through the solar system. Information is available regarding the International Space Station and the history of various types of air and spacecraft. The games and activities have five different skill levels and cover a variety of topics that appeal to students' interests in outer space and space travel.

NATIONAL GEOGRAPHIC KIDS

HTTP://KIDS.NATIONALGEOGRAPHIC.COM

National Geographic Kids is an interactive educational website where students can watch videos, look at photos, play games, read stories, and participate in polls. A variety of contests are available for students to participate in, including an annual photo contest. This site presents information on a wide range of different cultures, and includes arts and crafts activities and even recipes. Students can also find science experiments and information about energy efficiency.

JUST FOR FUN

NGAKIDS

HTTP://WWW.NGA.GOV/KIDS/KIDS.HTM

NGAkids allows students to learn about art history and technique through slideshows of famous works, such as John Singleton Copley's *Watson and the Shark* and Frank Stella's *Jarama II*. Parents can find family guides that encourage the discussion and creation of art, and tools like Brushter, the Collage Machine, and 3-D Twirler let students create their own art online.

PBS KIDS GO!

HTTP://PBSKIDS.ORG/GO

Students can play with their favorite PBS characters at this game-oriented offshoot of the PBS Kids site. There are a wide variety of interactive and educational games, including one called the Webonauts Internet Academy (http://pbskids.org/webonauts). In this game, students are introduced to the basics of Internet safety by learning the motto: *observe, respect, contribute*. Through this activity, students learn how to navigate the Internet. There is also a helpful section for parents and educators.

PEACE CORPS CHALLENGE

HTTP://WWW.PEACECORPS.GOV/KIDS

This game gives students the opportunity to work as Peace Corps volunteers in the fictional village of Wanzuzu. Students are asked to solve critical challenges to help the villagers make their home a better place. Issues such as water pollution, energy efficiency, and health care take the forefront as students learn about the work of the Peace Corps around the world. In this way, students become more aware of international issues while they enjoy an interactive problem-solving adventure.

THE PROBLEM SITE

HTTP://WWW.THEPROBLEMSITE.COM

At The Problem Site, students can play educational games and work daily puzzles, find interesting reference pages, and engage in fun problem-solving activities. There are word games, math games, strategy games, math problems, mystery quests, and many other free educational resources. Much of the site's content targets students in grades K–6, and the Junior section provides material specifically for preschoolers and early elementary school-age students.

PRONGO

HTTP://WWW.PRONGO.COM

Prongo offers interactive, educational games for students and is divided into sections for ages 3–6, 6–9, and 9–12. There is a quiz section as well as an abundance of math games and activities. Older students can use Wally's Stock Ticker to find out more about the stock market. Other features include e-cards, jokes, and brain teasers.

WEBRANGERS

HTTP://WWW.NPS.GOV/WEBRANGERS

WebRangers is the National Park Service's online Junior Ranger program for students of all ages. Here, kids can learn more about national parks and play more than 50 games related to this topic. In addition to learning about the history and current state of national parks, students can learn about basic outdoor survival skills that they could use while exploring the parks. They can also find information about becoming a park ranger and what a park ranger does at work.

JUST FOR FUN

MUSEUMS

THE BRITISH MUSEUM

HTTP://WWW.BRITISHMUSEUM.ORG/
EXPLORE/ONLINE_TOURS.ASPX

The British Museum offers a number of online exhibits and tours that focus on the art and history of different parts of the world. Exhibits are organized primarily according to geographic location. The majority of these collections focus on the art and tools of various civilizations and nations. This emphasis on artifacts and cultural ephemera allows students the chance to study how physical objects shape historical understanding of a particular culture. The art inspired by religion and spirituality in these collections is especially noteworthy.

CARNEGIE MUSEUM OF NATURAL HISTORY

HTTP://WWW.CARNEGIEMNH.ORG

The Carnegie Museum of Natural History offers online lessons via an interactive video conference program that allows students to ask questions and receive answers instantly in the fields of biodiversity, culture, and Earth science. Students can also explore 12 online exhibitions, which focus primarily on geology and paleontology but also include the experiences of Native Americans and the explorations of Lewis and Clark. This museum also offers the Traveling Classroom and Museum on the Move programs, the latter of which is tailored to students with special needs. These initiatives extend the museum experience to students in a more interactive, small-scale environment.

EXPLORATORIUM

HTTP://EXPLORATORIUM.EDU

Exploratorium is an interactive museum that aims to feed curiosity in science, art, and human perception. Its award-winning site contains more than 18,000 webpages that explore hundreds of different topics.

The online collections are particularly strong in the arts and sciences. This website also dedicates a section to the interests of teens.

LOUVRE MUSEUM
HTTP://WWW.LOUVRE.FR/EN

At the Louvre Museum's website, students can discover some of the world's most treasured pieces of art. Online tours allow viewers to explore virtual representations of select museum wings, while the Visitor Trails section (listed under Activities & Tours) presents collections of pieces by period, artistic movement, or theme. The site also hosts a variety of interactive modules in the section titled A Closer Look, which allow students to examine specific pieces of art in depth. This website also offers links to thematic mini-sites, which cover topics such as Babylonian art, the decorative and literary arts of Iran, and the rivalry between Titian, Tintoretto, and Veronese.

THE METROPOLITAN MUSEUM OF ART
HTTP://WWW.METMUSEUM.ORG

The official website of The Metropolitan Museum of Art includes teacher resources, an interactive gallery, and a searchable database. Students can search for particular pieces according to time period, medium, artist's name, location, or type. This website also offers interactive thematic timelines of art history. The kids section of the website links students to podcasts about art history and theory as well as family programs and activities. There is also a notable section regarding the science of art conservation.

NATIONAL GALLERY OF ART
HTTP://WWW.NGA.GOV

The National Gallery of Art allows students to explore its collection of paintings, sculptures, works on paper, photographs, and decorative arts through virtual tours, which can be chosen by school or medium. In-depth study tours are also available and can be chosen by artist or theme. Many of these online guides are also available as PDF

MUSEUMS

files. The museum's collection is particularly noteworthy for its Italian Renaissance pieces, including a significant number of works by Titian and Raphael.

SMITHSONIAN
HTTP://WWW.SI.EDU

The Smithsonian boasts of 137 million artifacts in its collection, many of which can be viewed online. Collections are broken down into art and design, history and culture, and science and technology categories, with subsets of each. The Smithsonian offers cultural programming year round, and certain centers, including the Smithsonian Latino Center and the Smithsonian Center for Folklife and Cultural Heritage, have their own websites that can provide further resources and information. A section of the website offers activities and other material specifically for kids and has a variety of materials to support classroom instruction. Under the Educators tab, teachers can find links to many curricular materials. For example, Smithsonian Source (http://www.smithsoniansource.org) has resources for teaching American history. Educators can easily search for primary source documents, photographs, or artifacts by historical topic. Smithsonian Folkways (http://www.folkways.si.edu/tools_for_teaching/introduction.aspx) provides lessons, resources, and interactive features for promoting cultural understanding through music. The list goes on with resources to support art, social studies, and science instruction.

MUSEUMS

MENTORING

INTERNATIONAL TELEMENTOR PROGRAM
HTTP://TELEMENTOR.ORG

The International Telementor Program (ITP) facilitates electronic mentoring relationships between professional adults and students in grades K–12. By emphasizing electronic communication as a means of mentorship, ITP hopes to expand the number of professionals able to serve as mentors. Most of ITP's programs focus on career exploration and college prep, with emphasis on the science, technology, engineering, and mathematics (STEM) fields. ITP utilizes Problem-Based Learning techniques and resources to encourage independent thinking within the framework of mentorship.

MENTOR
HTTP://WWW.MENTORING.ORG

MENTOR is a comprehensive site for mentoring support materials. This website offers resources to help start mentoring programs, to help adults become mentors, and to help students find mentors. The aim of this organization is to close the gap between the number of students who want a mentor and those who already have one. MENTOR is particularly noteworthy for its mentor programming and development resources as well as its professional development and training opportunities. The programs on this website emphasize student growth in academic skills, self-esteem, and career goals.

NATIONAL MENTORING CENTER
HTTP://EDUCATIONNORTHWEST.ORG/NMC

The National Mentoring Center (NMC) at Education Northwest offers resources to students in grades K–12. Among the resources are publications, forums, and a collection of FAQs and answers. The NMC offers training for mentors and funding for specific mentorship programs. The NMC also hosts specific resources for mentors working in

MENTORING

youth populations with special needs, such as students in the foster-care system and those with disabilities. The NMC also offers resources for faith-based mentoring initiatives.

LEADERSHIP

ACADEMY OF ACHIEVEMENT

HTTP://WWW.ACHIEVEMENT.ORG

The Academy of Achievement's mission is to "bring students face-to-face with the extraordinary leaders, thinkers, and pioneers who have helped shape our world." Students can explore a database of interviews with prominent individuals in the arts, business, exploration, public service, science, and sports. The Achiever Gallery showcases the Academy's inductees, and the Recommended Books section located therein provides a list of books that inspired current and past leaders.

AMERICA'S PROMISE ALLIANCE

HTTP://WWW.AMERICASPROMISE.ORG

America's Promise Alliance seeks to ensure access to fundamental resources necessary to enable young people to maximize their potential and give back to society. One of the organization's top priorities is ending the high school dropout crisis. Parent involvement is emphasized in developing students' potential, and a Parent Engagement Toolkit is one of many resources this organization provides.

CONGRESSIONAL YOUTH LEADERSHIP COUNCIL

HTTP://CYLC.ORG

The Congressional Youth Leadership Council (CYLC) selects students with outstanding academic skills and community leadership experience and offers them unique learning experiences. Students are invited to attend conferences at state, national, or global levels, where they can meet high-ranking government officials, diplomats, and other important figures. This organization offers students the chance to participate in behind-the-scenes, interactive academic environments while learning about government and policy making.

DO SOMETHING

HTTP://WWW.DOSOMETHING.ORG

Do Something encourages children and teenagers to take an active role in public affairs. This organization emphasizes the importance of volunteering with student-organized clubs. Students can browse through a list of causes and find opportunities to work toward effecting changes that they find important. There is also a listing of existing clubs that is searchable by state. This organization also offers Boot Camp programs for young community leaders and grants to help students with the start-up and growth of their own independent clubs.

FREE THE CHILDREN

HTTP://FREETHECHILDREN.COM

Free the Children is an organization that equips students with the skills necessary to become effective leaders who can make global impacts. The focus of this organization is to empower youth in order to increase activism and active citizenship. This organization focuses primarily on using education as a means to help underprivileged and exploited youth worldwide. Key issues are access to water, child labor, education, health, and poverty. Resources are available for student leaders on various forms of activism, event planning, and documentary making.

HUGH O'BRIAN YOUTH LEADERSHIP

HTTP://WWW.HOBY.ORG

The Hugh O'Brian Youth Leadership (HOBY) acknowledges and nurtures leadership potential in high school students. Schools nominate outstanding students to attend HOBY conferences and events, which then train them in leadership and activism. HOBY offers state leadership seminars and programs at the national and international levels; program alumni work as HOBY ambassadors at these events. The Volunteer Training Institute and the World Leadership Conference are two of the major initiatives that HOBY orchestrates, providing opportunities for students to expand their leadership skills and understanding of major issues.

NATIONAL YOUTH LEADERSHIP COUNCIL

HTTP://NYLC.ORG

The National Youth Leadership Council (NYLC) is an organization devoted to using community service to help students and their communities embrace multiculturalism. The NYLC's goal is to train and inspire students to make "a more just, sustainable, and peaceful world." Some notable projects sponsored by the NYLC are Project Ignition, which aims to promote teen driver safety, and Y-RISE, an HIV/AIDS prevention program.

NATIONAL YOUTH LEADERSHIP FORUM

HTTP://NYLF.ORG

The National Youth Leadership Forum (NYLF) offers students in grades 9–11 with academic and leadership talent the chance to explore specific career fields in a 6-day program. Students can focus on law and crime scene investigation, medicine, or national security. Enrollment requires nomination by a teacher or mentor and program locations and dates vary by focus area.

NATIONAL YOUTH LEADERSHIP NETWORK

HTTP://WWW.NYLN.ORG

The National Youth Leadership Network (NYLN) is specifically designed for students with disabilities; it aims to train these students to become leaders. The organization's focus is on self-advocacy. By encouraging students to become involved in policy making, the NYLN hopes that students can foster acceptance and multiculturalism. Emphasis is placed on building support systems and creating safe spaces. There are also specific resources designed to help students combat bullying and discrimination.

LEADERSHIP

YOUTH LEADERSHIP INSTITUTE
HTTP://YLI.ORG

The Youth Leadership Institute (YLI) seeks to give young people the power to get involved in their communities and create positive social change. The YLI offers students in California a chance to work with adults to address issues such as access to healthy food, educational equity, and civic engagement. This organization emphasizes the importance of self-expression as a catalyst for social change.

ONLINE CLASSES

CLASS.COM

HTTP://WWW.CLASS.COM

Class.com offers quality online classes for educators, parents, and students who need additional or different education instruction. In addition to traditional subject areas, this website offers classes in elective fields such as business, music appreciation, and photography. Study skills and career planning classes are also available, and there is a wide range of technology-oriented offerings, including classes on desktop publishing, digital imaging, and webpage design.

K^{12}

HTTP://WWW.K12.COM

K^{12} is an online learning service that offers classes for gifted and talented students as well as remedial and nontraditional students. These classes are available through online public schools, online private schools, or independent study. Classes are designed so that students can work at their own pace and advance whenever they are ready. The computer science and technology classes for high school students are particularly notable, covering topics such as image design, game design, audio engineering, and C++ programming.

UNIVERSITY OF NEBRASKA–LINCOLN
INDEPENDENT STUDY HIGH SCHOOL

HTTP://HIGHSCHOOL.UNL.EDU

The University of Nebraska–Lincoln's Independent Study High School provides young gifted students the opportunity to take online classes with students from many locations. Students can choose to take these classes full-time or as independent studies to supplement traditional schooling. The program is fully accredited by state, national, and international agencies. The website includes helpful information for parents who are considering this option for their children. This school empha-sizes college prep in addition to traditional subject areas.

THE VHS COLLABORATIVE

HTTP://THEVHSCOLLABORATIVE.ORG

The VHS (Virtual High School) Collaborative brings together hundreds of schools in order to offer classes to students who need advanced or remedial learning opportunities. High-school-level classes are avail-able specifically for gifted and talented middle school students. The focus of this website is on 21st-century issues and skills.

ONLINE CLASSES

CHAPTER 3

FURTHER READING

Following are listings of books that should prove helpful for teachers and students, respectively, as they navigate the online world.

BOOKS FOR TEACHERS

Ameis, J. A. (2006). *Mathematics on the Internet: A resource for K–12 teachers*. Upper Saddle River, NJ: Pearson/Merrill Prentice Hall.

Brooks-Young, S. (2010). *Teaching with the tools kids really use: Learning with web and mobile technologies*. Thousand Oaks, CA: Corwin Press.

Conn, K. (2002). *The Internet and the law: What educators need to know*. Alexandria, VA: Association for Supervision and Curriculum Development.

Cruz, B. C., & Duplass, J. A. (2007). *The elementary teacher's guide to the best Internet resources: Content, lesson plans, activities, and materials*. Columbus, OH: Pearson/Merrill Prentice Hall.

Green, T. D., Brown, A., & Robinson, L. (2007). *Making the most of the web in your classroom*. Thousand Oaks, CA: Corwin Press.

Greenlaw, J. C., & Ebenezer, J. V. (2005). *English language arts and reading on the Internet: A resource for K–12 teachers*. Upper Saddle River, NJ: Pearson/Merrill Prentice Hall.

Hawthorne, K., & Sheppard, D. (2005). *The young person's guide to the Internet: An essential website reference book for young people, parents and teachers.* London, UK: Routledge.

King, K. P., & Gura, M. (2009). *Podcasting for teachers: Using a new technology to revolutionize teaching and learning.* Charlotte, NC: Information Age.

Lerman, J. (2005). *101 best web sites for elementary teachers.* Eugene, OR: International Society for Technology in Education.

Lerman, J. (2005). *101 best web sites for secondary teachers.* Eugene, OR: International Society for Technology in Education.

National Center for Education Statistics. (2000). *Teacher use of computers and the Internet in public schools.* Washington, DC: National Center for Education Statistics.

Provenzo, E. F. (2005). *The Internet and online research for teachers* (3rd ed.). Boston, MA: Pearson/Allyn & Bacon.

Reich, J., & Daccord, T. (2008). *Best ideas for teaching with technology: A practical guide for teachers, by teachers.* Armonk, NY: M. E. Sharpe.

Roblyer, M. D. (2006). *Starting out on the Internet: A learning journey for teachers.* Upper Saddle River, NJ: Pearson/Merrill Prentice Hall.

Smith, G. S. (2007). *How to protect your children on the Internet: A road map for parents and teachers.* Westport, CT: Praeger.

Warlick, D. F. (2007). *Classroom blogging: A teacher's guide to blogs, wikis, and other tools that are shaping a new information landscape.* Raleigh, NC: Lulu.

BOOKS FOR STUDENTS

Bailey, D. (2008). *Cyber ethics.* New York, NY: Rosen Central.

Harris, A. R. (2010). *Txt me l8r: Using technology responsibly.* Edina, MN: ABDO.

Jacobs, T. A. (2010). *Teen cyberbullying investigated: Where do your rights end and consequences begin?* Minneapolis, MN: Free Spirit.

Porterfield, J. (2010). *Conducting basic and advanced searches.* New York, NY: Rosen Central.

Rabbat, S. (2010). *Find your way online.* Ann Arbor, MI: Cherry Lake.

Selfridge, B., Selfridge, P., & Osburn, J. (2009). *A teen's guide to creating web pages and blogs.* Waco, TX: Prufrock Press.

Wan, G. (2007). *Virtually true: Questioning online media.* Mankato, MN: Capstone Press.

REFERENCES

American Library Association. (1998). *Information literacy standards for student learning.* Chicago, IL: Author.

Christakis, D. A. (2009). The effects of infant media usage: What do we know and what should we learn? *Acta Paediatrica, 98,* 8–16.

Corporation for Public Broadcasting. (2002). *Connected to the future: A report on children's Internet use.* Retrieved from http://www.cpb.org/stations/reports/connected

Fish, A. M., Li, X., McCarrick, K., Butler, S. T., Stanton, B., Brumitt, G. A., . . . Partridge, T. (2008). Early childhood computer experience and cognitive development among urban low-income preschoolers. *Journal of Educational Computing Research, 38,* 97–113.

Gerzog, E. H., & Haugland, S. W. (1999). Web sites provide unique learning opportunities for young children. *Early Childhood Education Journal, 27,* 109–114.

Jackson, L. A., Samona, R., Moomaw, J., Ramsay, L., Murray, C., Smith, A., & Murray, L. (2007). What children do on the Internet: Domains visited and their relationship to socio-demographic characteristics and academic performance. *CyberPsychology and Behavior, 10,* 182–190.

Leu, D. J., Jr., Kinzer, C. K., Coiro, J. L., & Cammack, D. W. (2004). *Toward a theory of new literacies emerging from the Internet and other information and communication technologies.* Retrieved from http://www.readingonline.org/newliteracies/leu

Mendoza, J. A., Zimmerman, F. J., & Christakis, D. A. (2007). Television viewing, computer use, obesity, and adiposity in U.S. preschool children. *International Journal of Behavioral Nutrition and Physical Activity*. Retrieved from http://www.ijbnpa.org/content/pdf/1479-5868-4-44.pdf

National Association for the Education of Young Children, & Fred Rogers Center. (2012). *Technology and interactive media as tools in early childhood programs serving children from birth through age 8.* Retrieved from http://www.naeyc.org/files/naeyc/PS_technology_WEB.pdf

Schneider, J. (2009). Besides Google: Guiding gifted elementary students onto the entrance ramp of the information superhighway. *Gifted Child Today, 32*(1), 27–31.

Schrock, K. (2002). *Teaching media literacy in the age of the Internet: The ABCs of web site evaluation.* Retrieved from http://school.discoveryeducation.com/schrockguide/pdf/weval_02.pdf

Siegle, D. (2005). Six uses of the Internet to develop students' gifts and talents. *Gifted Child Today, 28*(2), 30–36.

Wells, J., & Lewis, L. (2006). *Internet access in U.S. public schools and classrooms: 1994–2005* (NCES 2007-020). Washington, DC: National Center for Education Statistics, U.S. Department of Education. Retrieved from http://nces.ed.gov/pubs2007/2007020.pdf

ABOUT THE
AUTHORS

Frances A. Karnes, Ph.D., is professor of curriculum, instruction, and special education at The University of Southern Mississippi and director of the Frances A. Karnes Center for Gifted Studies. She is widely known for her research, writing, innovative program developments, and service activities in gifted education and leadership training. She is author or coauthor of more than 200 articles and coauthor or coeditor of 71 books on gifted education and related areas. Dr. Karnes is the former president of The Association for the Gifted and is the founder and first president of the Mississippi Association for Gifted Children, and she has served on the board of the National Association for Gifted Children. Honors include a Faculty Research Award, granted by The University of Southern Mississippi Alumni Association; an honorary doctor of education degree from her alma mater Quincy University; and an award presented by the Mississippi Legislature for outstanding contributions to academic excellence in higher education. She has received the Power of One Award bestowed by the governor of Mississippi and was named one of 50 female business leaders by the *Mississippi Business Journal.* In 2007, she received the Lifetime Achievement Award from The University of Southern Mississippi.

Kristen R. Stephens, Ph.D., is an associate professor of the practice in the Program in Education at Duke University. Prior to this appointment, Dr. Stephens served as the gifted education research specialist for the Duke University Talent Identification Program. Over the years, she has coauthored numerous books and coedited the Practical Strategies Series in Gifted Education, a series comprised of more than 30 books on issues pertinent to gifted child education. Dr. Stephens served on the board of directors for the National Association for Gifted Children, the North Carolina Association for Gifted and Talented, and the American Association for Gifted Children.